A Matter of Death and Life

D. L. KLINE

Balboa Press books may be ordered through booksellers or by contacting:

Balboa Press
A Division of Hay House
1663 Liberty Drive
Bloomington, IN 47403
www.balboapress.com
1 (877) 407-4847

Print information available on the last page.

ISBN: 978-1-5043-8044-7 (sc)
ISBN: 978-1-5043-8046-1 (hc)
ISBN: 978-1-5043-8045-4 (e)

Library of Congress Control Number: 2017907587

Balboa Press rev. date: 03/19/2018

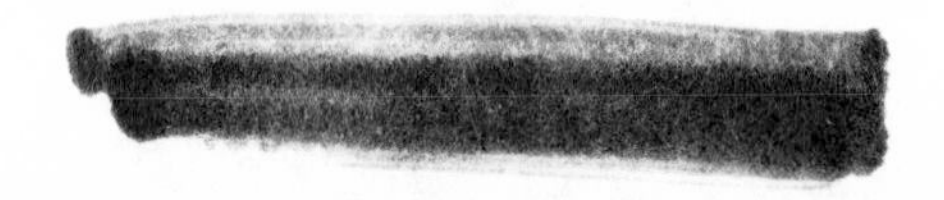

Dedication

For Pookie and the Poodle, always …

1 Introduction

Until a very few years ago, I was just an ordinary guy, living a fairly ordinary life; work, eat, and sleep like everybody else. I always had a passing interest in what some folks would call the paranormal. You know, psychics, past lives, stuff like that. But I had never really taken a lot of time to think about that type of thing. Then one day I was home from work during the week and happened to be watching *The Montel Williams Show.* His only guest that day was a psychic named Sylvia Browne. Hearing her talk about the other side and seeing her make connections between audience members and departed loved ones not only caught my interest but started to change my whole way of thinking.

I had a few of Oprah's aha moments during that hour, and afterward couldn't do enough reading and learning about psychic phenomenon, especially when the teaching was done by Ms. Browne. Unfortunately for the planet at large, she transitioned home a short time ago, but she left us her body of work in the form of many books and writings.

While I kept reading and learning about all things psychic, I never felt a strong and personal connection to the other side until I had the opportunity to undergo past life regression with an amazing psychic/healer named Barb Ruhl. I met Barb through my wife, and she led me on several regressions until at one session, we both encountered an entity from the other side. He told us his name was Jasper and that he was my primary spirit guide.

Jasper figures strongly in all the things I write about because he is not only a guide but a teacher as well. His methods of instruction are not exactly orthodox, but he acts the way he does to get and keep my attention. You'll be hearing a lot more about him as we go along.

Once I was directly reconnected with Jasper, not only did my channel to the other side reopen, but my life has never been the same. Barb has become my mentor but also a fellow student, both of us trying to learn and understand everything all the souls on other side are trying to teach us.

Believe me, it hasn't been easy. Some of the truths the other side has revealed have not only contradicted my early religious training but also things about dealing with life that I was taught to believe since childhood. I always thought of God as an angry, punishing entity far removed from caring about what went on in my life. My religion told me he existed, but mostly to judge me after I died and consign me to hell if I hadn't followed the many rules laid down by the church in his name.

Through my interactions with my friends at home, I have come to know there no such thing as hell, God consists of nothing but unconditional love, and we are all directly connected to that love without need of any clergy to intercede. Writing this and my other books has been as much about my personal learning and spiritual growth as it has been about sharing what I'm learning with others.

Which brings us to the subject of this book, death. And more important, life. I'm very happy to be able to tell you everything the other side has taught me so far about those two subjects. So let's get started.

Death is another of those words, like *reincarnation* and *meditation*, that has so many meanings to so many people that it almost takes on a life of its own. Ironic, isn't it, that the word *death* has a life of its own?

For something that is a complete illusion, death has become so ingrained in our psyche that it not only supports a $20 billion a year funeral industry, it has become a nearly complete obsession with some people. Or more correctly, the fear of death has become an obsession.

We even have given death a form, though not a face, in the personage of the Grim Reaper, a guy in a black hoodie, carrying an old-school farm implement. Really? That's what we are supposed to be terrified by? Surely, someone could come up with a better embodiment of death.

As I said, the real obsession is not with death itself; it's with the fear of death. Not knowing when or how it will happen, or if it will be painful, and most especially, insecurity about not knowing what, if anything, happens to the essence of you, your soul, after you "die" is what people are afraid of. Would it help you to know that you plan your death at the same time you're planning your life so that it can help you achieve your learning goals? Probably not. I believe the biggest fear surrounding death still is, without question, what happens after the fact.

Owing to the influence and teachings of our old friend organized religion, people are unsure. Organized religion has always held that it, and only it, knows the secrets that unlock the doors to heaven and hell, and only by believing certain church dogma and performing certain required acts, usually involving the transfer of money from you to the church, could it allow you to access heaven.

Hell, conversely, has pretty loose admissions standards. Basically anything that falls outside the requirements outlined by the various religions to get you into heaven can get you a one-way ticket to that place. Then purgatory, limbo, and any number of other fantasies come into play. It's exhausting just trying to keep track of it all.

The problem is our feelings about death are so complex and come from concepts that extend so far back into the "mists of time," as they say, that we have difficulty sorting out what to believe. Just like the ancient Romans, whose culture still pervades our own, we simply have too many things available to believe. The Romans took pieces of religion from all the people they conquered and fused them into their own existing dogma.

They eventually had so much religion that they ended up with no religion, just a hodgepodge of differing beliefs.

We all know in the early years of Christianity, the Romans had some big problems with the idea of another religion. One of the reasons they couldn't trust Christianity was because it was new to them. They believed that unless a religion had some age to it, it must be only a superstition, and as such, Christianity was not deserving of respect.

They also had issues with Judaism because of the one God thing. But the reason they destroyed the main Jewish temple in Jerusalem was not because they had anything against the Jewish religion. It was because the Jews were in a near constant state of rebellion against the Empire. The fact that the temple was full of gold and jewels also helped in making the decision, of course.

The point is, our beliefs about death and the afterlife are so old and so wrapped up in the myths and stories the Romans borrowed from any number of cultures they conquered to create the Empire, that we have trouble getting to the kernel of what is perceived on earth as the truth at the center of it all. It also doesn't help that this kernel is an illusion because death, as defined by organized religion and modern society, doesn't exist.

The purpose of this book is to help you sort out your own beliefs about death by providing perhaps a new perspective with information I and others have received from the other side.

Nobody ever "dies." When this body you are currently inhabiting ceases to function, and an earthly life can no longer be maintained by it, you, the real you, your soul if you will, simply leaves that body and returns to your home in the dimension next to this one. Jasper says I should invent a word to replace *death* because like the word *God*, it's taken on so much religious stigma that its true meaning has been lost. I told him sure, I'll get right on that. I mean, introducing a new word into the English language to replace an old one, how hard can it be?

My best effort would be to substitute the word *transition*, but as always, that's not quite good enough for Jasper. Borrowing from the world of the theater, Jasper says death compares more to an intermission. The curtain comes down on one life, there is a brief pause, and when the curtain goes up again, there is a new set.

The star of the show may be playing a different role, but nothing changes all that much. So I asked, *If things change on stage during intermission, wouldn't that be considered a transition to a different play?* And then he said … I will spare you the entire conversation, but seriously, these are the things that go on in my head.

The point is, just as the old hymn says, "There is no death, though eyes grow dim." The true essence of who we are lives forever, just moving back and forth between home and the earth plane for purposes of learning and growing. So our obsession with death and dying is a complete waste of sometimes large chunks of what little time we have here on earth. We need to, as Cher said to Nicholas Cage in *Moonstruck* after she slapped him in the face, "Snap out of it!"

The words in the title of this book, *A Matter of Death and Life*, are arranged that way because the first, and shortest, part of the book talks about the illusion of death. The second, and larger, part talks about the much more important topic of life here on earth and explores in greater depth how and why we pick the things we choose to experience before we incarnate.

I don't expect anyone to blindly accept what I tell you in this or my other books. I encourage you to be skeptical and question everything. I do expect, however, that you give serious thought to everything you read and not dismiss it out of hand because it flies in the face of many things you have been taught to believe. As Sylvia used to say, take whatever feels right to you, and leave the rest. If you can remain open to new ideas and concepts, you'll have more help than you can imagine in incorporating a new normal into your life to aid in your spiritual growth.

People always ask, "What is the purpose of life?" The answer to that age-old question is a simple one: spiritual growth. That is the one and only reason we incarnate here. We are not required to do so. We want to because like steel burnished by fire, living a life in the negativity of this planet and coping with all that it brings makes our souls grow stronger.

My desire for this book is to help many people move forward in their spiritual journeys by sharing all the insights I've been given from the other side. But if it turns out that I've only helped myself and a few others, it was still worth the effort.

2 In the Beginning

It's only been about three years since I had the psychic awakening that started my spiritual journey in earnest. In the sixty years before that, I was slogging along through life like the vast majority of people, bound up in the guilt, fear, and anger (emphasis on the anger) generated by my interactions with family, jobs, church, friends and acquaintances, and the world at large. Somewhere in my forties, I figured out that organized religion just didn't have answers to the problems I was encountering, especially after my wife developed a near-fatal illness.

I don't think I ever had serious doubt about the existence of God, but I certainly couldn't continue to believe in the angry, vengeful, punishing God with all the rules that were being shoved down my throat by the church. Just looking around, I could see what might be called minor miracles happening almost daily, including my wife's recovery from her illness. Why would the same God who helped perform those miracles that improved, enhanced, and sometimes even saved lives then send you to hell for eternity for some infraction of "the rules"? Talking about bipolar personality! It just didn't make sense to me. It still doesn't make sense to me.

I questioned and searched for years until I became aware of the late Sylvia Browne. I became an avid fan of hers, tried to catch every TV show she appeared on, and eagerly read her many books. She taught me many things, not the least of which was to keep a sense of humor about the whole deal of living out an earth life to further our learning and soul growth. And even though Sylvia maintained her ties to her religion, she still was brave enough to teach that there is no such thing as the devil or demons, and there is no such place as hell. She used to say if you want to see hell, just look around; you're living in it.

She also taught us that God is not exclusively male. The source of unconditional love also has a female side for the balance necessary to keep the universe on an even keel. In short, she taught us many wonderful things before she went home, but I still felt something was missing. The connection was incomplete for me. Sylvia gave us an exercise in one of her books that was supposed to help us connect with our spirit guides, and I tried it time and again without success. For whatever reason, it just wasn't working for me. I felt like I was putting together a jigsaw puzzle, but I was missing a few important pieces.

So I struggled along, like so many people do, coping with life as it came at me the best way I knew how. Sometimes I made the right decisions, sometimes not. I always felt there was something more, that I was something more than a person to whom things were always happening, a victim instead of the star in my own little play.

Then, when I turned sixty and was beginning to feel my life was pretty much over, and the remaining twenty or twenty-five years I had left would go on much like the previous sixty, I had my psychic awakening. I can truly call it an awakening because the whole process has been like waking up from a bad dream.

I went through the same feelings we all have when waking up. At first, you're groggy and not sure where you are. Then, as you begin to wake up, you're not quite sure if what you remember really happened or if it was a dream. Finally, when you do become fully awake and aware, you realize it was just a nightmare, and none of it was real—even though at times you were terrified, and your heart was beating fast. Once you're fully awake, you might even chuckle about being so scared about nothing.

That metaphor is a perfect way to describe our lives when we are incarnated. These lives we pick are just scenarios we play out to help us learn what we want to learn about ourselves. They are not real, and the person we are while we are incarnated is not who we really are. He or she is just a piece of us that becomes an actor playing a role for a short time.

Unfortunately, we can be easily convinced that this is who we are, and this is all there is to life due to the amnesia we impose on ourselves about the reality of the other side when we are incarnated. Our subconscious is also easily convinced that what we're experiencing is real in the same way it thinks dreams and nightmares are real, causing you to have that rapid heartbeat and sweat on your brow when you wake up from them.

I have had interactions with people on the other side, including my mother and mother-in-law, that have convinced me people assume personalities here while they are incarnated that are absolutely nothing like those they have when they are at home and can be who they really are. We all assume different personalities when we incarnate for the purpose of learning and teaching.

My mother, who didn't enjoy her most recent life much, told me she treated me the way she did because I asked her to as a way of teaching me forgiveness and tolerance. Out of love, she, like all of us have at one time or another, was willing to completely change her normal personality to help another soul grow. Of course, she was learning at the same time, but her main purpose in the life she shared with me was to help me learn the things I mentioned before. When I see her now, I don't see the woman I sometimes actually hated. I see a being of pure love and joy, which is her true nature.

After my friend Barb helped me to reopen my channels of communication with the other side, I could see not only the whole of home but the actual place I live while I'm there and not incarnated. I saw a lot of my friends and was shown and told what my job is there, which is to help souls that are going to reincarnate plan their earth lives to provide the maximum potential for learning and growth.

Even without being given all the details I received about my life at home, it would have been enough to know there is more to me and to life than just what we're living through now. I had always been taught, of course, that heaven existed, and if I managed to make the cut, I would get there after I died and be assigned a cloud, wings, and a harp to strum for eternity.

Even when I still bought into the whole organized religion thing, the thought of floating around on a cloud until the end of time seemed like an incredible bore. That's why I was ecstatic to find out that I had a job there, like we all do. Life without a purpose, to me, is just an existence. Even if you feel your only purpose is to drag yourself to a job you hate to be able to pay rent and buy food, at least it is some kind of purpose.

Everything I was learning was pointing me in one direction, and that was to dealing with all the guilt, anger, and fear I accumulated in this lifetime and some I carried over from some of my past lives, hoping to finally resolve those issues in this life. I wrote extensively about how to deal with those three ugly stepsisters in my second book, so rather than rehash all that information, I'm just going to tell you about how coping with them improved my life.

I will freely admit, and Jasper will happily point out, that I still carry some guilt, anger, and fear. But compared to what I was dragging with me three short years ago, it's next to nothing. All three of those negative emotions are so closely related and intertwined that even I have trouble isolating what was fear or anger or guilt because anger comes from fear, and guilt comes from anger. I can't say it any better than Franklin D. Roosevelt when he said we have nothing to fear but fear itself. You can't hope to put a smackdown on all three ugly stepsisters if you can't figure out what you're afraid of.

There are hundreds of things that people fear, but the root of all fear, I think, is not knowing what the future holds. It starts out at a very early age with fears of abandonment, strangers, and so on. It continues through the school-age fears of not making or keeping friends, not passing tests, not getting asked to the prom, or getting accepted into college. Adult fears make up a very long list, so you can fill in your own blanks here. But they concern jobs, money, relationships—all that stuff—up to and including the fear of death.

The thing that helped me most in moving past all my fears was finally knowing and understanding I planned this life for my own benefit, so why would I plan something that was going to hurt me in a way I couldn't recover from? This is one of the biggest issues I have with the teachings of organized religion. Churches teach that when you encounter challenges in your life, God must be testing or punishing you. This, of course, makes you afraid of God and reinforces the notion that the rules made up by the church are the only things that can save you from eternal punishment.

As I have said over and over, the Creator is composed of nothing but unconditional love. He does not test or punish. In fact, he has so much unconditional love for us that he is willing to let us plan our lives and then sits back and lets us live them, no matter how hard it is for him to watch us stumble around, making mistake after mistake.

You can't possibly be a victim in your own life because you planned to experience all these things before you even incarnated. It's called personal responsibility, people. Accept it. You knew when you were planning your life that you were strong enough to endure whatever you planned, so suck it up, buttercup.

The point is, no matter how horrible you think your life is, you planned it that way to learn something. So instead of putting on the sackcloth and ashes and going into full-on martyr mode, take a step back from your situation, and try to figure out what you're supposed to be learning, be it patience, tolerance, endurance, or the biggies—self-love and self-esteem. Once you recognize your scenario as the learning experience it is meant to be, you can stop wallowing in your feelings of victimhood and move on without fear to the next thing you are supposed to be learning.

3
To Die For

In my last book, *The College of Spiritual Knowledge*, I wrote that I couldn't believe it had been fifty years since we first heard William Shatner say, "Space—the final frontier," in the opening credits of the original *Star Trek* television series.

While outer space may still be considered an external frontier humanity has yet to conquer, none of us need to leave this planet or even our homes to find important internal frontiers that still need to be crossed while living out our current incarnations here on earth. Death—or more correctly, our understanding and feelings about the death of our physical bodies—is a major new world that most of us need to explore. So let me borrow a little from Shatner and subtitle this chapter "Death—The Final Frontier." Let's boldly go to a place we don't like to talk or think about and come out on the other side of it with a greater understanding of our thoughts and feelings about death, where they come from, and hopefully, how we can once and for all get over it!

As I stated in the introduction, death, or what most people consider to be death, is a complete illusion. It simply doesn't exist. I know, I know. I can hear you saying that all you have to do is watch the evening news, and you can see that any number of people have died in any number of gruesome ways. Or you can read the obituaries in the daily newspaper, if anyone out there still reads newspapers. And, of course, we've all watched various family members die and have attended way too many funerals. In those instances, and more, we've all seen what is considered death.

But what we've witnessed is actually the inability of the bodies we currently inhabit to continue functioning. The real part of us, the essence of who we are, can never cease to exist. That part—let's call it the soul to give it a name familiar to everyone—is eternal and immortal. When the bodies we are living in can no longer sustain themselves or cease to function by trauma or disease, we leave them behind and return to our real home on the other side for some detox and R and R. Then comes lots of planning to come back in other bodies and do it all again.

I discuss this further as we go along in this book, but before I get too far ahead of myself, let's backtrack a little and examine how and where our beliefs about death originated. As those of you who have read my other books know, I can't resist throwing in a history lesson or two when I have the opportunity. So here comes one.

Death is as old as life. Life and death come as a set, so even our cave-dwelling ancestors must have realized that when a body ceases to function, the person who inhabited it has gone. Over time, prehistoric people developed the idea that when the body dies, the essence of the person in there goes somewhere. So they started to have more and more elaborate burials with ever more numerous and varied things included in the graves they thought the deceased might need in this new place they were going to.

As ancient people came to believe that supernatural beings controlled everything in the physical world from unseen and magical places, they developed the belief in gods who controlled the underworld and dealt with the souls of the departed. The ones we are most familiar with in Western cultures are, of course, the Greek Hades and the Roman Pluto. The Romans also had a separate god of death, Libitina.

Some beliefs about death held by organized religion today, such as souls going to a special place in the underworld to be punished for myriad reasons, are hand-me-downs from Greco-Roman ideas. But among all the ancient civilizations, the rock stars of the whole death and afterlife belief system thing are, without a doubt, the ancient Egyptians.

The Egyptians took the whole preparation for death belief system to a level unseen before or since. They had not one but two gods, Anubis and Osiris, just for the handling of all aspects of death and the next life. They perfected mummification so that the body could be used in the afterlife, and they had that well-known *Book of the Dead*, one of the greatest moneymaking schemes of any organized religion ever. The book described what happened to as you journeyed from this life to the afterlife, and the priests sold the same or a similar book for huge sums of money over and over again, telling each buyer it was written specifically for them.

That book was also the world's first cheat sheet. Not only did it reveal the questions you would be asked along the way in your afterlife journey, it gave you the correct answers to enable you to pass through the several gates between this world and the next. It even described what you needed to do while in life to pass the ultimate test, which was when your heart was weighed against a magic feather.

If you hadn't been a good person, helpful and kind to your fellow humans during your life, your heart would be heavier than the feather and tip the scales in the wrong direction. You would be devoured immediately by a giant crocodile. Game over. If your heart was lighter than the feather, you immediately entered paradise and lived happily ever after.

Who knew that the old sayings about feeling light as a feather and your life hanging in the balance are over five thousand years old? Interestingly, and just as an aside, eight of the Ten Commandments from the Bible have nearly the same wording as the directions in the *Book of the Dead* for living a good life.

As I stated before, death is a complete illusion, but most people in this dimension see death as the final act in the play that is their current lives. That idea, for any number of reasons, is so ingrained in the modern psyche that people believe it even if they identify as members of an organized religion with afterlife as one of its tenets. As a society, we have become so death obsessed that we allow our preoccupation with the whole subject to overshadow the real purpose of our being here, which is to expand the spiritual side of our lives to help in our souls' growth.

Add up in your head the number of phrases or words that describe being born. Other than *coming into the world, being born* is pretty much it. Now think over how many words and phrases there are to describe death. Start with *buying the farm, kicking the bucket, taking a dirt nap,* and *biting the dust.* Then think of simpler ones, like *curtains, demise, expiration, parting,* and *passing.* In the medical field, we use terms like *CTB* (ceased to breathe) or *boxing,* as well as the old standby *croaking.* Then you can go religious and use *entering eternal rest, going to your heavenly home,* or *resting in the arms of God.*

The list goes on and on. Not only are the words we use for leaving this life many and varied, they are far more colorful and entertaining than the two or so terms we have for the process of coming into this world.

It's as if we, as a people, are saying, "Yeah, you were born. Big whoop; we all were." Maybe it's because there are only two ways for each of us to be born—vaginally or by cesarean section. But the ways we choose to exit this plane of existence are different for each of us because we are all individuals on our own spiritual journeys.

Even though we all plan how and when we will transition back to the other side at the same time as we plan our current incarnations, we develop anxiety about how we will make that change because we've all seen the many and varied ways people die, especially in the age of the Internet.

I'm sure those of you who have read my other books have wondered when Jasper, my main spirit guide and homeschooling teacher, was going to chime in, and the answer is now. He says that part of the attraction for us to incarnate on this planet, other than the fact that we are adrenaline junkies, is the chance to experience what death feels like, including all the emotions associated with it. More specifically, to experience living with the fear of death.

Since the essence of who we are is immortal and eternal, there is nothing like death on the other side. So souls come to earth for the chance to feel finite.

Jasper says earth incarnation is like a giant roller-coaster ride in that way, and this planet has the same kind of appeal as a great amusement park. It is sort of the Universal Studios of the real universe because, apparently, death of the physical body is rare.

But back here on earth, people can let the fear of death—particularly the fear of not knowing what happens to you after you die—become an obsession. Like many people with a huge fear of death, their lives can amount to a complete fixation on death and dying, so much so they stop living while they are still in their physical bodies. Your soul can't possibly be growing and learning if the only things you think about 24/7 are death and dying, whether it be your own or someone else's.

When you suffer the loss of someone close to you, it's painful and can derail your life for a time. But if ever there was a completely wrong description of someone transitioning to the other side, it would be *lost*. You can lose big at the blackjack tables, you can lose your train of thought (especially at my age), or even lose your car keys, but no one who exits a physical body and returns home to the other side is ever lost. They know exactly where they are. They are at home and happy. They often try to let us know they are those things if we stop feeling sorry for ourselves long enough to look and listen for the messages they are trying to send.

I know this is starting to sound like a lesson in tough love, and I'm not proposing that everyone abandon the grieving process after someone close to them transitions. Going through the stages of grief is a very human and normally healthy thing to do. But there must be a limit. There must be a time when you start to develop mechanisms for coping with feelings of loss because that is one of the most valuable lessons most of us come here to learn and work on.

One of the most important things to learn during your grieving is to identify exactly why you are grieving. I know you're thinking it should be obvious; someone close to you just died. But if you are feeling sorry for your dearly departed because you think he or she is dead, you can stop that train of thought in its tracks. Your loved one is home, happy, and reunited with everyone he or she knows who transitioned before your loved one and have not already reincarnated. Be honest with yourself; admit most of the grieving you're engaged in is mostly about feeling sorry for yourself and feeling the absence of your loved one.

It's perfectly natural to feel that way for a time, and it will be a different amount of time for every individual. But if feeling sorry for yourself starts to take on characteristics of victimhood that lead to full-blown martyrdom, it's gone way too far. You have to stop and think—indeed, know at a soul level—that all this was planned by you and your loved one before you both incarnated. You have to do your best to work through and conquer all these feelings in this lifetime.

If you look around any old, established graveyard, you will see an amazing variety of tombstones and crypts, with statues of all kinds and big stone monuments dedicated to people who were never in those graves to begin with. In fact, two of the seven ancient wonders of the world, the Great Pyramid at Giza and the Mausoleum at Halicarnassus, were both elaborate tombs built to house the bodies of dead kings. I am not a fan of devoting so much space and money to the housing of dead bodies, so I'm greatly encouraged that in recent years, more and more people are choosing cremation instead of internment. You can even have your ashes turned into diamonds and made into jewelry for those who remain after you have transitioned.

In the past, Christian teaching always held that the body had to be preserved so that it would be available when all the dead rose from their graves at the second coming of Christ. I think that belief is not as widely held today, especially with the growth in knowledge of reincarnation.

Even if you don't let your life become filled with the fear of death, many people still have a sort of love affair with the idea of death. Does anyone really believe NASCAR fans flock to races to watch cars that seldom make a right turn go around in a circle? No, they go consciously or subconsciously hoping for a massive car wreck and then maybe, just maybe, someone will get killed. I'm not saying race fans wish death on someone, but that morbid fascination with death is certainly a driving (excuse the pun) factor behind attending a live event of that kind. Jasper would like to point out here that some deaths are planned by the individual to serve a positive purpose. To stay in our racing analogies, Dale Earnhardt's death improved safety requirements for all race car drivers. A serious message from Jasper? Wow.

Let me summarize this chapter by going back to one of my favorite movies of all time, *Moonstruck*, for which my girl, Cher, won her Oscar. Toward the end of the film, some of the family is gathered in the living room, and Olympia Dukakis, playing Cher's mom, says to her husband, "Cosmo, no matter what happens, you're still going to die." That's the takeaway from this chapter as well as the whole book, and it bears repeating. No matter what happens, we're all going to die, and since we planned how and when it is going to happen when we planned our lives, there is no need to fear it or obsess about it.

Live your life. Even if you don't believe me about planning your death, you still have no control over it, outside of not doing anything stupid or dangerous to precipitate the event. So don't waste any time dwelling on it, and most especially, don't form an emotional attachment to it.

I find myself telling people to "be careful" or "be safe" when we part, like if I don't tell them that they're going to walk into oncoming traffic. But doing that is just a small example of our cultures' morbid fascination with death. Remember what the guides have been trying to teach us all along: our lives here are just like videogames. We play them out to move up levels, and when one virtual life is over, we have the opportunity and choice to have another one. Just don't waste the one you currently have worrying about things you can't control and will happen anyway.

Live and love the experiences you're having when you're having them and for as long as they last. Rest assured you can have as many more as you need or want with every incarnation. Remember that if your family insists on having a tombstone for you after you transition, your entire life will be represented by that dash between the date of your birth and the date of your so-called death. So make the most of it.

4
Sorry for Your Loss

I know what you're thinking. It's easy for the spirit guides who are providing us with much of this information about death, living in an environment of no negativity, surrounded by the unconditional love of the Creator, and with access to all the knowledge in the universe to tell us not to fear or obsess about the death of our physical bodies. Unfortunately, or in reality fortunately, we are the ones incarnated on this planet and dealing with all the emotions that go along with that state of being.

Because I was emotionally abandoned by my parents at an early age (all part of my life plan and agreed to by my parents and me before I incarnated this time), I sort of had to raise myself. To say I was, and still am to some degree, socially awkward is one of the great understatements of all time. As a result, I never really knew what to say to people who just experienced the death of a loved one. I finally settled on, "Sorry for your loss," mostly because it's quick, easy to say, and covers a lot of scenarios. Now that I'm fully aware of what happens when we transition to the other side, it seems disingenuous to keep saying it.

I will keep saying it, however, because family members in the receiving line at a funeral home aren't ready to hear, "Woohoo!

Let's party because your loved one just moved up another level in his spiritual advancement." I do expect to hear that and many other similar things at my memorial service, so be prepared if you attend and are expecting the usual funeral nonsense. It will not be happening, but a party with my favorite food and drink will be. But since that isn't going to happen for a lot of years, let's move on.

Let's see if we can get some perspective on grieving and loss. First, even if you are still attached to the teachings of organized religion on death, know that no one is ever lost while transitioning to the other side. We, and they, know exactly where they are after they leave this dimension. They are at home. The whole scenario is exactly like leaving for work every day. You go to your job, and when you're done, you go home with the certainty that your house and family are going to be there exactly as you left them that morning.

Those things don't disappear just because you are not physically present. The same holds true for the other side. Not to mention that incarnating for a life on this planet is the hardest job you'll ever have. And I realize organized religion has tried to convince us of the existence of a hell as an alternative to being able to go home after you die if you haven't followed all the rules and regulations. But even if you buy into that nonsense, at least you know your departed loved one went somewhere, right?

Not to minimize anyone's pain or grief at being separated from a loved one by a transitioning, but that pain is really a self-inflicted wound. The feeling of loss is all on this side because that negative emotion, like all negative emotions, simply doesn't exist on the other side. As I and so many others have written, the soul whose loss you're grieving knows exactly where it is, sees you clearly, and hears you plainly. If the soul knows you are open to the possibility, it will even try to contact you to let you know things are fine. I used to watch the late Sylvia Browne when she appeared on television, and the number one question nearly everyone asked was, "Is my deceased mother, father, wife, husband, child okay?" With great patience, I think more patience than I could muster, Sylvia answered time after time, "Yes, they're fine, they're all fine, and much happier than we are."

People need to be reassured about that all the time. As someone who has only been able to be in direct contact with souls who have transitioned for a little over three years, I get it and can relate. I guess my point is, if you focus your anxiety on your departed loved ones and how they are, you're worrying needlessly. They are all home and just fine.

Your focus should be on coping with your grief and using it as a learning tool to enhance your soul growth. That is the purpose of experiencing grief or any other negative emotions: to develop the coping skills needed for dealing with it and then moving on so you don't have to repeat the same lesson in the next life. At least that is how things are supposed to work. But as ever and always, we have the gift—and curse—of free will come into play.

Although we take the time to meticulously plan all the details of our lives before we incarnate, we can't plan for how the incredible negativity of this dimension, coupled with our free will, can derail those plans and send us off on unintended side trips. Let me use another life experience of my own as an example. As you may or may not know, this whole spiritual journey of mine started with my desire to do past life regressions with my psychic friend, Barb Ruhl. One of the first lives we regressed to was one in thirteenth-century England. I was a man named

Robin Locksley, on whose life the Robin Hood legend came to be based. I described how Robin had a best friend named Will Short, who helped him in his work of robbing the rich and giving to the poor. What I was advised by the guides to leave out of the narrative when I wrote my first book is that Robin and Will were a couple and hopelessly in love.

That little detail was revealed to me when I saw them kissing passionately after one of the robberies. At any rate, Will was framed by the local authorities for sodomy and put to a hideous death, which Robin had to watch. After the execution, I saw Robin leave the castle and walk into the forest, sobbing. I thought that was all I would be shown of that life until a few weeks ago, when I was having a session with Barb. Jasper told us we needed to see the rest of Robin's life. So we went back to our old way of Barb putting her hands on my temples so she could better see what I'm seeing. Jasper told us to go to the end of Robin's life. After focusing on that, we could see him as an old man, or at least old for the period, with long gray hair and a beard.

He was living as a hermit in a cave in the forest, where he had apparently gone after witnessing Will's death, and never left. His grief and sense of loss were unending and took over his life to the point he could no longer follow his plan. This meant he never learned the rest of the things he was supposed to learn after coping with his grief and loss. Barb and I watched as Robin left his body and transitioned to the other side. Because he, through his free will, made the unconscious decision to live nearly half his life in a state of severe grief and mourning, Robin had to undergo some special healing after he got home. He also had to add coping with loss to the things he would have to deal with in future incarnations.

We go into the details of how that all happens in a future chapter, so for now, let me just say that once you commit through your life plan to learning how to cope with any life scenario, just like in any binding contract, you must do what you said you would do, even if it takes more than one life to do it, and even if you did or didn't consciously decide not to pick up those coping skills. That's why it's always best to deal with whatever comes along in life as it is happening. Delaying doesn't absolve you from learning to cope.

About a year ago, I was shown another of my past lives that took a turn similar to my Robin life in coping with loss. It was near the end of the Civil War, and I was a Southern plantation owner named Rhett near Charleston, South Carolina. Unfortunately, my plantation didn't raise cotton; it raised slaves, the sale of which made me extremely wealthy. I was rich enough to buy my way out of fighting for the Confederacy and was living a very good life. I was preparing to attend a ball to celebrate my engagement when there was a surprise attack by the Union Army. The place where the ball was being held was blown up, killing many people, including my fiancé.

I was so overcome with grief and survivor's guilt that I left everything I owned behind and headed west. Every time civilization caught up with me, I just went further into the wilderness until I ended up in a remote area of the Rocky Mountains, living in a small cabin.

The last scene I observed from this life was my death. Just as in my Robin life, I wasn't very old (I just looked old) and died of exposure during a blizzard. Once again, I went to the other side full of a huge feeling of loss. And again I had to undergo healing for that once I got home. Somewhere between that life and this one, I seem to have at least improved if not perfected my coping with loss skills because none of the things I've lost in my current incarnation have made me want to go live in a cave. At least not yet.

By letting me see those two particular lives—Robin and Rhett—the guides showed me and all of us that letting grief and loss take over your life brings the learning process to a screeching halt. In both instances, I might as well have physically died with my loved one because spiritually, that is essentially what happened, and the coping tools I anticipated developing never evolved in either of those lives.

What I'm trying to get across is we all suffer feelings of loss and despair when grieving for a friend or relative that has transitioned. But after learning and knowing that no one who goes home is lost but is right where he or she should be, it means we often create our own victimhood by retreating into an all-encompassing state of grief.

Of the many things I want you to take away from all of my books, one of the biggest is that there are no victims or martyrs here because of the life planning we do prior to our incarnations.

However, any of us can easily make ourselves into victims or martyrs by blaming anybody and everybody for how we feel and react to life situations. Don't do that to yourself when it comes to grief and loss. Work through it, cope with it, and move on. As Dolly Parton used to say, "Get down off that cross, honey. Somebody can use that wood."

5

Grandma's Gonna Die

When I was a young, hot-shot, big-city nurse in an intensive care unit (ICU) back in the last century, I worked in a surgical ICU. Its director was an internationally known expert in the mechanical ventilation of lungs damaged by disease or trauma. Because he was so well known in his field, young doctors came from all over the world to work under him and learn his methods of treatment. Since it was in a large city, the hospital often received patients from smaller hospitals in the surrounding area who needed surgery but were at a high risk for postoperative complications due to coexisting health issues.

One such patient I remember was a man in his early eighties. He had a number of chronic health problems and came to our hospital to have an abdominal aortic aneurysm repair. Just by way of a quick anatomy lesson, the aorta is the large artery that comes directly out of the heart and supplies oxygenated blood to the entire body. An aneurysm is a weakening in the wall of a blood vessel that can expand like a balloon. Just like a balloon, it can also burst under pressure, and in the case of the aorta, can cause massive internal bleeding and a rapid death. If the aneurysm is found before it ruptures, it can be surgically repaired. But it is major surgery, and in older people with other health issues, it can cause serious problems postoperatively.

And so it was with this gentleman. He survived the initial surgery but wasn't able to have his breathing tube removed. So he spent several days in the ICU on a ventilator as his condition deteriorated. He went into kidney failure, liver failure, was placed on dialysis, and had multiple blood transfusions. About ten days after his surgery, he died from multisystem organ failure without regaining consciousness.

The reason I remember this gentleman from nearly forty years ago is because of the reaction of the young doctor from Ireland who happened to be on call the night this man went into cardiac arrest and died. After the code blue was called off and the patient was pronounced dead, this young doctor said to me, "In Ireland, we would never have done surgery on this man. We would have sent him home and told him to sit on the front porch and enjoy whatever time he had left with his family around him."

At the time, being a gung-ho, young, health-care provider who believed absolutely everything that could be done to prolong life should be done, I thought Ireland must be a pretty backward place to just send people home to die. Now, forty years later and having witnessed this scenario played out time and again, with usually the same results and often without the knowledge and consent of the affected patient, I can see the wisdom in the Irish approach. I hope their attitude hasn't changed over the years.

The simple fact is Grandma's going to die, and so is Grandpa. So are we all. It's a major piece of the mechanism that keeps the whole universe functioning. The physical bodies we choose to inhabit for a short time have a shelf life, just like all perishable organic matter. When that predetermined point in our earth lives comes, the essence of who we really are leaves this body behind and transitions back home, usually to begin planning within a short time for our next trip into another physical body.

The point I'm trying to make is that with all the advancements that have been made in all areas of medicine, especially in the last hundred years or so, it's possible through medication, treatment, and surgery to help people live longer, healthier lives. That is a wonderful thing. The longer we can live full, functional lives, the longer we have to work on fixing all our emotional issues, so we can focus on expanding our spiritual growth in our future lives, not working through the same emotional scenarios over and over.

People, in general, are living twice as long as they did in the even recent past, so our opportunities for soul growth while incarnated have also doubled as time has marched on.

With all that being said, I'm certain nearly everyone alive today has gone through—or knows someone who has gone through—the emotionally traumatic decisions that must be made for a loved one who can't make his or her own decisions at the end of life. People of a certain age are so used to there always being another available pill or treatment that will keep prolonging the inevitable, they think it's necessary to stay in these physical bodies even when it is clear the body is barely functioning, and any type of quality of life has long since gone away.

This is the real dilemma we all face when deciding on that next medication or that next surgery for ourselves or someone we're providing care for. Which is more important: quality of life or quantity of life? Everybody, I think, wants to have a rich, full life and then die in their sleep at a ripe old age. In reality, very few people plan to have that type of life because without at least some struggle and hardship, there isn't much spiritual growth and learning going on. And without growth and learning, there isn't much point in putting yourself through another incarnation.

So most of us choose to sweat and struggle our way through one incarnation after another. Because those incarnations are lasting longer and longer, and the world seems to be getting harder and harder to live in, we tend to develop health issues related to our striving, like high blood pressure, diabetes, and obesity. Luckily, they can be treated with medication and lifestyle changes so that we all don't die of heart attacks and strokes at an early age. Unless, of course, that's the type of death we planned for ourselves.

But all these new drugs and treatments are like the proverbial double-edged sword. We can use them to increase the quantity of life, but all too often, by doing that, we must sacrifice quality of life. I recently saw a television commercial for a new drug touted for its ability to dramatically increase the length of life of a certain type of cancer patient. But if you read the very fine print at the bottom of the screen, it only increased the survival rate from something like six months to nine months.

So for an extra ninety days, is it worth the expense and the risk of side effects? Some people would say unequivocally yes; life must be prolonged no matter what. How about if I told you that you will spend those last three months draining your bank account and debilitated with nausea, vomiting, and diarrhea. Still worth it?

I think more and more people are saying no, it's not worth it. Just as in my story of the Irish doctor, people are deciding to have the highest possible quality of life for whatever amount of time they have left, rather than trading that for a longer quantity of time that may be spent feeling sick and doing nothing but going to doctor after doctor, seeking treatment after treatment.

I'm not saying life isn't precious and meant to be treasured. Of course it is. But every individual must decide what kind of life they want to lead: happy, independent, and doing pretty much what they want, or spending their days feeling lousy and shuffling between doctors' appointments.

Which brings me back to the point of this chapter, which is, Grandma's gonna die. When you have an older person, or any person in your life who can no longer make decisions for himself or herself, and you are the designated decision maker, you must understand to the core of your being that eventually, that person will die. And it's okay; it's all part of the grand plan. But when the time comes, will you be willing to let nature take its course, or are you going to insist absolutely everything that can be done be done, in spite of all the evidence showing you that it's time for your loved one to go?

Statistics from a CMS study done on Medicare patients who died between 1992 and 1999 tell us that greater than 25 percent of a person's total Medicare expenses are incurred in the last year of life. Years ago, they used to call it the $100,000 funeral, but that was back before a funeral could actually cost that much money. Anyone who has worked in health care for any length of time can tell you exactly why that number is valid, and it's not necessarily because of the patient. It's because family members are overtaken by some kind of hysteria about Grandma dying.

She can't, she just can't die. Even if she wants to. She needs another surgery, another treatment. She needs dialysis and a ventilator. She needs to spend the last month of her life unconscious and in an ICU bed with tubes stuck in every available orifice. She needs a tracheostomy and a feeding tube. Of course, all the things I just mentioned can be billed for by the medical establishment, so more often than not, they will be happy to indulge the family.

I'm absolutely certain that if Grandma could communicate at this point, or could have before all the decisions were made to go down that road, she would say, "Take me home, and let me die peacefully in my own bed, with people I care about around me, not surrounded by nurses and beeping machines." I have made it abundantly clear to my family that if I get to the point where I can't make decisions for myself, there are to be no heroics. No breathing tubes, no ventilators, no CPR. When time's up for this incarnation, time's up. I've done what I came to do, and it's time to let me go home and start over.

I hope in this book I can help at least some people get over this fear of death that is so pervasive in our society today. Death isn't the end of anything. It's the beginning of the next chapter in the never-ending story of the lives we live in the unfathomable expanse of the Creator's universe that surrounds this tiny little planet we call home.

At this point in my journey, I have seen enough people cross over to the other side and spoken with enough people there, including the beautiful soul who agreed to be my mother for this lifetime, to know that the actual crossing over is not a bad thing. Whatever pain we are in before we die is gone when we go home, and often gone before we go. There is no pain or discomfort with the actual leaving of the body. Just a feeling of peace and indescribable happiness.

A good friend's mother transitioned not long ago. During her earth life, she was what could only be described as a mean and nasty person. When she transitioned, she was so happy to be going home and back to being her real self that I saw her running there with her arms in the air and shrieking with joy, relieved that a life she had not enjoyed was over.

In summary, when you are faced with a situation where you have the choice of letting someone go or using extraordinary measures to keep the individual's physical body functioning, ask yourself who you are making the decision for. I think in a high percentage of cases, the decision maker is acting in his or her self-interest because of the inability to let Grandma go. Well, guess what? If Grandma is unconscious, she's already spending most of her time on the other side, so pull the plug, and let nature take its course.

6

Long Day's Journey into Day

We've talked a lot about all the emotions surrounding the transitioning of a loved one to the other side. Now let's get into the mechanics of what actually happens when someone "dies."

Even though there are hundreds of ways that our physical bodies can stop functioning and make it necessary for our essences to leave this dimension and return to the one next door, they all can be placed in two basic categories: fast and slow. In the fast category, you have any sudden death caused by trauma, murder, suicide, heart attack, stroke, and so on. Basically, any death that might make people say, "But I just saw him, and he looked fine." In the slow category, you can include old age, chronic illness, and life itself because it always results in death.

No matter what type of death you had planned for yourself, the one thing they all have in common is that at the actual time of transitioning, all pain stops. Even if your death up to that point was protracted and painful, the transition itself is quick and painless.

All the suffering you may have experienced was put there when you planned your current incarnation for your learning. Once you go through as much of it as you need or want to, it ends.

You may need a little extra cocooning time once you get home to help get past the negativity that a long and painful death engenders, but on the other side, it all becomes just a memory and a life lesson learned.

One special exception that can fall into either the fast or slow category, though it is more common in the fast death category, is the near-death experience, or NDE. NDEs have gotten a lot of attention in the last few years, with several best-selling books being written on the subject. One of my favorites is *Proof of Heaven*, by Eben Alexander MD. In it, Dr. Alexander, a neurosurgeon and the ultimate skeptic, has his own NDE and returns with a completely different outlook on death and life. I highly recommend reading his book.

NDEs occur when someone's physical body stops functioning for a brief period, and the individual's essence, or soul, starts the transition to the other side. During that time of transition, people often report seeing a tunnel or a bridge they must cross, with a shimmering white light at the other end. They also often encounter deceased relatives or "heavenly beings," who tell them it's not their time and that they must return to their physical bodies and finish out the life they are currently living. Details may change from person to person, but the overall experience is very similar for the many thousands of people who have had an NDE and then decided to tell the story.

In a recent session with Barb, the guides confirmed everything I just talked about but added a few details of their own that I am happy to share with you.

First, even though everyone on the other side intellectually understands the fear of death that we have while incarnated, they just don't get what it feels like to experience it in this environment. Jasper says the death of your physical body should be celebrated with a party, not a funeral. It's a happy time, like retirement. You've finished your work and get to go home and relax for a while. He says if you notice, a lot of people transition around their birthdays and the winter holidays. The reason for that is those are both happy and exciting times on earth, and people transitioning are excited to be going home.

No matter how much fear and sadness there is on the outside, the inside is happy to be going home. Now you'll never be able to listen to Perry Como sing, "There's no Place Like Home for the Holidays," without thinking about it in a whole new way.

All transitions start the same way. It's just that people having an NDE are stopped short of going through the shimmering white curtain that marks the boundary between the earth and home, while a soul who is transitioning will pass completely through.

But let's back up a little bit, and as the incomparable Julie Andrews sang in the *Sound of Music,* let's start at the very beginning; a very good place to start.

Let's start by talking about the actual physical location where people die. I really hate the term "deathbed" because it has so many bad memories for so many people. So let's call the place where you leave your physical body behind the "transition spot." Already sounds like more fun, doesn't it?

Not to belabor the point, but where and how you're going to transition is chosen by you during your life planning. Depending on your predetermined choices, your transition spot may not necessarily be a bed. It could be anywhere, so that makes a generalized term like "transition spot" even more applicable. So to give this explanation in a step-by-step manner, let's say we're in our chosen spot, our transitioning is under way, and we're either alone or surrounded by any number of friends and family.

I'm sure there are some people out there, though no one I know, who have been with somebody while he or she transitioned who haven't heard the person say he or she saw deceased relatives, God, or someone right before they die.

I was talking with a friend whose father transitioned a short time before, and she told me about the final days of his earth life. His physical condition had deteriorated to the point where the only words he could say were "yes" and "no." As his family gathered around him, they noticed he was looking at the ceiling, like he was seeing things there.

When he was asked if he was seeing something, he answered yes. When asked if there were people there, again he said yes. They then asked him if he was seeing his departed mother, and again the answer was yes. They asked him if he was seeing his departed father. And again, he said yes. Then, when asked if he was going to join them, he said no. They thought that was a good thing because it meant he wasn't leaving just yet and that he could answer questions with something other than the word *yes*. Even though he did transition the following day, his no answer was technically correct at the time the question was asked.

I remember when my father was dying of lung cancer over forty years ago. The evening before he transitioned, he told my mother he had to go. When she asked him where he was going, he said, "To be buried." Kind of macabre but truthful, nonetheless.

I think I could pretty much fill an entire book with accounts of things people who are transitioning have said and what the people around them heard and saw at that special time, but I'm sure you get the idea. I'm also sure all of you have either experienced the same thing or know someone who has, so I'm not going to belabor the issue further.

The important thing to know and understand is when people are in their transition spot, the things they see and say are not caused by the effects of drugs, disease, or lack of oxygen to the brain. Those are the stock explanations given by nonbelievers, skeptics, and the medical establishment for all the things that happen at the time of transition.

The experiences transitioning souls have and talk about to people around them when physically possible are happening in real time. They may be skewed a little by the person's religious beliefs. And they may change from person to person because the transition team on the other side always tailors the experience to the individual to make it as easy and atraumatic as possible, but they are, without question, happening. These are some reasons people in the Western Judeo-Christian tradition often see someone they interpret as being God or Jesus as they pass through the tunnel. They don't fear going toward that type of celestial being.

Jasper just popped in, dressed in flowing white robes and with a long white beard, to let me know that when I transition from this current incarnation, he will be playing the role of God just to make me feel safe. He actually looks more like Charlton Heston when he was playing Moses in *The 10 Commandments*, but anytime I compare him to a movie star, he is elated. My motto is, Happy Jasper, happy life. And like I still wouldn't recognize that face behind a big white beard.

The point he is trying to make, I think, is that we all have a transition team on the other side made up of five or six people you love and trust and are already there. Just like everything else, there is a plan in place to make the first part of your transition home as easy as possible. The team will include a loved one or two that have already transitioned, maybe your parents or spouse, and then at least one of your guides.

Because you may not immediately recognize your guides as you begin to transition, and because your guides are living in the pure unconditional love of the other side, they may often appear to your still human eyes as glowing or golden forms. So, many times, they will be mistaken for angels or some other heavenly beings based on the transitioning souls' earthly religious beliefs.

Before we get any further into the details of the transitioning process, let me repeat the "Story of O" chapter from my first book, *Suddenly Psychic*. My mother-in-law, big O to many who knew her, transitioned in December 2014. At the time, I thought she was going at Christmastime just to screw up the holidays for all the family. But Jasper has since taught me the real reason so many people transition around that time of year, as I've already discussed, so I don't hold it against her.

In case you haven't read my first book, or haven't guessed, my mother-in-law and I butted heads for the entire forty plus years I knew her, but I now know that she was trying to teach all of us who interacted with her patience and tolerance, and in the end, she gave me the tremendous gift of watching her transition, which I'm going to relate here.

On the Wednesday before Christmas 2014, my wife received a call from the nursing home where her mother was a resident, letting her know her mother's passing was coming soon, so she left to go there the next day. Because I was working, I couldn't leave until the following Saturday. While I was driving, I saw my father-in-law, who had already transitioned, pop into my head. I asked him why he didn't just take my mother-in-law home with him. He laughed and said he could never tell her what to do, which was very true.

I found out when I got to the nursing home that the time I saw my father-in-law was the time that Big O transitioned, so he really was there to help her.

During the actual transition, I saw a shimmering white wall or curtain, which I have come to learn is the barrier or boundary between this dimension and the other side. Then I saw a much younger and thinner O step through the boundary with a very surprised look on her face. She was wearing one of those seersucker housedresses that button up the front, which were popular in the early 1960s, mostly as a validation to her children, who recognized it as something she used to wear all the time. She then realized she was walking, after being confined to a wheelchair for the last four years of her life, and laughed out loud while rubbing her now pain-free knees.

I then saw a sister-in-law of hers who had already transitioned come forward and hug her, and she was greeted by the rest of the souls assembled there. I didn't recognize anyone else, and the whole thing seemed kind of blurry and fast-forwarded. The last thing I saw was my mother-in-law and father-in-law walking away arm in arm.

While the whole story is fascinating to me, even more fascinating is that my wife's brother and his wife were present at her bedside during the whole transitioning, and they saw the same startled expression on my mother-in-law's face as she was leaving this dimension that I saw as she arrived on the other side at the same time, all providing more validation.

So with many thanks to the Big O for sharing her transitioning, let's get back to the details of how the whole thing works.

We're in our transitioning spot, whether it be a bed in a hospital, extended-care facility, or at home, or in a car about to run into an eighteen-wheeler, or in an alley somewhere, looking at a gun being fired at us. However and wherever we have predetermined in our life plans that are going to leave this dimension and go home, we are there. Our physical bodies cease to function in one of the myriad ways that can happen, and the essences of 99.99 percent of us leave our physical bodies and begin the transition to the other side.

The other 0.01 percent of souls are so attached to something here on earth that they don't make the transition and become, for a time, earthbound spirits or what people call ghosts. The topic of earthbound spirits deserves its own chapter, so we're going to skip over it for now and move on to what happens to the majority of us who go home to the other side in the regular fashion.

Let's talk about that famous tunnel. Nearly everyone who has had an NDE has spoken of the tunnel of light that appears before them. Some have also seen a bridge leading to a white light, but the common denominator seems to be a pathway of some kind going forward into a bright white light, which is that shimmering curtain separating the earth plane from the other side.

Jasper, as always, is ready to explain things in a way our puny human minds can comprehend. He says think of the passage as a long hallway, like a jetway when you're boarding a plane. It has a moving walkway, so you can either walk at your own pace or ride along slowly; again, just like at the airport. The hallway has what are kind of like flat-screen TVs at intervals along the walls, playing different scenes from the earth life you are exiting. This accounts for that "My whole life flashed before my eyes" feeling that people who have returned to their earthly lives have talked about.

Some souls take time to look at the images as they cross over; some don't. Once you get home and reacclimated, you will have plenty of time to review your just-lived life, so it doesn't matter how much of your transitioning time you spend here. Jasper says mostly people who have died from an extended illness or old age are the ones who take the time to really look at the screens. Others are in such a hurry to get home that they blow right past them.

As you move down the hallway, you encounter the five or so people I talked about before. While they are communicating with you at this point, it's up to you to make the decision about going back into your physical body. Most of us decide to continue through the white curtain and end our current earth lives. But there are some who decide they haven't learned all they incarnated to learn or haven't done all they intended to do and want to go back.

I also believe some people have written an NDE into their life plans so that they can come back to educate everybody on the whole process, or at least those people who are ready to hear about it.

One very important point I would like to make here is that all these decisions—when and where to transition, if you will have an NDE and return, all the way back to whether you incarnate in the first place—are made by you and you alone. We're going to get into why people choose certain lives and deaths in a future chapter, but it makes me crazy when I hear people say things like, "Why would God let that happen?" or, "Why doesn't God just take him or her?" That is not the Creator's role in any of this.

The Creator has nothing but total unconditional love for you. He exhibits it by standing back and letting you do what you feel you need to do for the growth of your soul. As I have often said, the idea of a God who punishes and tortures people for his own amusement comes down to us from the beliefs of the ancient Greeks and Romans and has no place in the reality of how the universe functions.

But back in the tunnel of light, we've met our transition team and we're deciding whether to go home or come back to work on things we haven't finished learning. If we decide to come back, that is the end of the story for now. We go back to our earth lives and continue as before. If we decide we're done with this incarnation, we continue with the team. We go through that shimmering white curtain, separating the earth from home, and into the process of reacclimating to our real lives that start when our tethers to our physical bodies are severed. So this might be a good time to talk a little about our spiritual tethers.

A lot has been written about our spiritual tethers by many authors, but the tethers are basically just fine ropes composed of vibrational energy that are attached to us when we incarnate to keep us connected to the other side and to the earth while we're here. Tethers provide links between our essences, or souls, the other side, our physical bodies, and the energy of the earth itself.

Writers as diverse as Sylvia Browne and Shirley Maclaine have described seeing a silver cord attached to their bodies around the area of the solar plexus, or heart chakra, that is particularly visible during an out-of-body experience. Barb and I were discussing the tether, and she said that she had always seen it as an energy that flowed down the spinal column and legs and then out of the body and into the earth to keep us grounded and connected to the earth energy. Then the other side chimed in with the explanation that the tether is actually in two pieces.

The part that runs from the other side and through the heart chakra is what keeps your essence and physical body connected to each other and to the other side while you are here. It then continues through you, running down your spine and legs, to provide an anchor to this planet, also just while you're here. It's this two-part system that allows your essence to astral travel and return to the other side while you're sleeping to sort of recharge your batteries and keep alive the soul memory that we are all much more than the confining bodies we live in while maintaining a connection to the physical body and the planet itself.

When we pass through the shimmering white boundary, the last thing that happens is the severing of the tether at the heart chakra. Our bodies stay here and rot back into the earth while our souls are on to bigger and better things. That tether to the earth energy is also the reason people enjoy nature and being outdoors while incarnated. That link keeps us connected to the essence of the planet and provides a feeling of being connected to the bigger universe at large.

I read recently that scientists have determined there are substances in the soil that work as well as drugs like Prozac in relieving depression. Maybe we should all make time to play in the dirt on a regular basis. No wonder kids are always so happy! Seriously, though, what you are doing by connecting with nature in any way is allowing the earth's energy to flow through that tether and make you feel more connected with and better about life in general.

Now that the guides have gotten us through the tunnel and told us how we sever the tether that keeps our essences connected to our physical bodies, they're going to let us see behind that shimmering white curtain and discover the next step in our journey to resuming our real lives on the other side. So, onward and upward, or onward and sideways, or onward and whichever way you perceive yourself as transitioning.

7

Honey, I'm Home, and I've Had a Hard Day

We've gone through the famous light tunnel, severed the tether to the physical bodies we were using in our most recent incarnations, and arrived at our real home on the other side, where we were greeted by some of our already transitioned friends and relatives and our guides. Now what?

Once the initial excitement of being home again and in the company of your nearest and dearest starts to settle down, a lot of things need to happen before you can fully resume your real life.

Something that I had never considered because of my puny human mind, of course, was that while on earth, one's infinite essence is contained and confined in the meat sacks we wear as bodies. We must be spiritually tethered to them when we're incarnated to keep us from leaving them behind while sleeping or meditating. It's during those times that our souls sometimes cross over to the other side for a little mini vacation, so we don't get so claustrophobic from being confined that we can't function on this planet at all.

Jasper, my ever-present and sometimes annoying spirit guide, says that because we go from the heavy, low-vibration atmosphere of the earth when we cross over to the high-vibration atmosphere of unconditional love on the other side fairly quickly, returning souls are treated like deep-sea divers who risk getting the bends if they come to the surface too rapidly. Just like divers, we're going from a dense, high-pressure atmosphere to a lighter than air kind of place. So after our initial meet and greet, we go to an area where the light is low, the colors around us are all muted, and the atmosphere is very thick, almost like a fog.

It's at this stage of our transitioning that people often suffer a period of confusion, especially if they are coming from a life that was heavily involved with organized religion. They'll be looking around for St. Peter with his keys to the pearly gates, asking where the throne room is so they can be judged. And most especially, they ask where God is. They expect to see all these things.

Of course, the pearly gates and the judgment throne were created by organized religion as a control measure. But the question about the location of God has some validity. The Creator, as I've written before, is not an old, white man with a long, white beard sitting on a throne. That's more accurately a description of the statue of Jupiter Optimus Maximus, the chief god in the Roman pantheon, or of a mall Santa Claus.

If you wanted and needed him to, the Creator would appear to you in that form. On the other side, his essence is everywhere. His unconditional love is pervasive, surrounding us like the air we breathe on earth. It's very difficult for us when we're incarnated and surrounded by all the negativity of the earth dimension to remember or imagine what it feels like to be bathed in unconditional love. The closest we can come to having that feeling while on earth, I think, is when we are babies and small children with an extremely loving family. But here again, we lose the memory of that as we grow older, just as we develop the amnesia we have about life on the other side. When we get home, we must reawaken those senses that allow us to feel the unconditional love of the Creator all around us.

To help accomplish that, we are sort of cocooned at this particular step to give the returning soul a feeling of being swaddled, like a newborn, which provides a feeling of safety and comfort. It helps to lessen the confusion caused by going from a confining human body to the absolute freedom of being in a state of only positive energy and love.

Jasper says I usually end up spending a significant amount of time in this area when I go home. For whatever reason, this part of the transition can be difficult for some people. It's what I think astronauts must feel like when they leave the earth and go to the zero gravity of the space station. It takes time to adjust to that feeling of not being physically constrained in any way.

In earth time, souls can be cocooned like this for days, weeks, or months. Even though Jasper is pretty cavalier about the process when I'm going through it—he says he spends a lot of time filing his nails and rolling his eyes—the enormity of the transformation the returning soul has to undergo to readjust and recalibrate to the higher vibrational level of home can't be minimized.

This process is never taken lightly because every soul is precious and has its own individual needs. It takes as long as it takes, and your primary guide, along with healers, will watch over you the entire time you're going through it. Just as an aside, I know people sometimes wonder why their loved ones who have transitioned don't give them any signs that they are okay for extended periods of time.

This cocooning process, which is not unlike being bundled up in some kind of soul-replenishing wrapper at an expensive spa, is often the reason. Some people can breeze right through it, while others, like me—according to Jasper—can take a significantly longer time to adjust.

The other guides are saying that the higher your vibrational level during your earth life, the less time you need to spend cocooned when you transition home. So maybe when I transition this time I can spare poor Jasper the long vigil. He says the only part of the cocooning process he enjoys is when I'm finally coming out of it because it's like watching Mike Myers as Austin Powers coming out of his deep freeze, minus the extended time at the urinal. He says I look like a newborn calf—all shaky, gawky, and falling down a lot. If my condition can provide some amusement for him, it is certainly worth enduring.

After we've been cocooned for however long it takes to recalibrate to the higher vibrational level of home, we emerge, not literally as butterflies, but with the same kind of feeling a caterpillar turning into a butterfly must have. We go from the confinement and limitations of the human bodies we occupied for our three score and ten here on earth and return to our natural forms on the other side.

Those forms can be a range of things, from something we would clearly recognize as human, to a sort of outline of a human shape, to the puffballs that I talked about before, like my friend and guide John, to the well-known orbs of light people frequently capture on film when they are "ghost" hunting. Whatever form we take at home, we must relearn the feeling of being free energy and interconnected with every other essence in the universe, without the limitations of the human body.

Let's just stop here for a minute for some further explanation of the last paragraph. I know a lot of you are thinking, *The old boy has finally gone off the deep end.* A few years ago, I would have thought that myself. What I can tell you with absolute certainty is that all this information comes directly from the guides on the other side, and most of the time I'm not writing these books as much just writing down the things they want us to know at this point in human development.

I can honestly tell you I have never had the type of imagination that could make this stuff up. That would take an author of the caliber of J. K. Rowling, which I am certainly not. Believe me, after all I have seen and been shown by my guides and others on the other side in the last few years, I have absolutely no doubt that what they want me to write is true and correct.

My only doubts come from thinking that many people just aren't ready to hear and accept this new information. But time and again, the guides have told me that those who are ready to accept it will, and it doesn't matter about the others. They will come around in time, so forge ahead.

Okay then, forging ahead. When we transition home, nearly everyone we initially encounter will be in human form to lessen the feelings of strangeness accompanying the return. Those of us, like Barb and I, who work in what I call shipping and receiving—that is, helping people plan their lives and to heal from any emotional trauma endured while incarnated—often stay in human form. Appearing that way assists people coming and going better adjust to both those things. Jasper says he always keeps his human form because he couldn't bear to look like every other puffball or orb of light in the universe.

Have I mentioned before that one of the reasons I usually have self-esteem issues when I incarnate is because Jasper likes to keep it all for himself on the other side? I think he convinces me that I need to work on my feelings of self-worth in nearly every lifetime just because he enjoys holding all the self-esteem and watching me struggle without any. Now he's giving me the pouty face, so where were we? Ah, yes, the forms we take when we transition home.

The basic human form is most common in the areas where people are coming and going because that is what they need and expect to see. In this area, we can also take on a form that is sort of like a shadow outline of a human body; you know someone is there, but it doesn't have any real features. I know, sounds kind of spooky looking, but a lot of souls take this form when they are still in the early planning stages of their next incarnation. It gives them a feeling of being human before they have made the selections of gender, skin color, height, weight, all those very specific details that must be worked out after we decide to come back for another go-round.

Also in this area of the other side, we can take the giant puffball form, which might best be described as looking like a dandelion after it has gone to seed. This is the form, as I said before, that my friend and guide John likes to assume when he's there. I'm not sure of the purpose of this form, other than it seems to be a halfway measure between the shadow form and the orbs of light. The first time I encountered John, he came across as a very no-nonsense kind of guy. He said he thought taking a human form just for the sake of looking like everyone else was just silly. I guess the purpose is to provide a visual shape that is acceptable to souls who are still reacclimating.

The orbs of light form may be the one most often adopted by those souls who are not planning an earthly incarnation anytime soon, or who never incarnate here at all. I know it may be disturbing to some people to think the human body is not the permanent form we take, but think about it. Human bodies may be wonders of engineering and chemistry, but they are rather frail things, easily damaged or destroyed, and reliant on the right temperature, atmosphere, and amount of sunlight to survive.

The human body must spend one third of its time in an unconscious state just to be able to make it through the other two thirds of its lifespan. And there are thousands of chemical reactions that have to occur constantly just to keep the thing functioning. If the reactions go don't take place exactly the way they are supposed to, it can lead to disease and/or death. Not to mention that this body has an extremely short shelf life, relatively speaking. It's for all those reasons that we must live so many lives just to learn anything.

But it's also for all those reasons that we get to live all those lives and learn so much. I guess you could say the physical body is a blessing and a curse. If we want to live on this planet and in this dimension, it's one of the forms we need to assume. However, when we're not in that physical body and take on the orb of light form, oh, the places we can go, and the things we can do! I'm going to leave an explanation of that until we're done with learning about how we transition into our real lives.

So to sum up the action so far, we've come through the tunnel, severed the tether that connected us to our physical bodies, had our first brief meet and greet, and then went through as much cocooning and healing as needed to get our vibrational level reacclimated to the one at home. What's next? We're getting closer to starting the process that allows us to deal with all the things we learned during the life we just lived. But even before we do that, we have to take care of any physical or emotional trauma we suffered and took home with us.

We now go to the area where healers like Barb work to determine exactly what and where our psychological wounds are and how best to treat them. Everyone is taken into a beautiful room filled with crystals of all shapes, colors, and sizes. You lie on a table in the middle of the room while healers arrange the crystals around you that will provide the necessary energies to "detox" you from all traumas you encountered on earth and then took home with you.

The crystals absorb the negative energy from your essence and replace it with positive energy to restore your vibrational level to 100 percent of what it was before you incarnated. Before you can review your just-lived life impartially and without self-judgment, you have to be completely free of any negativity that might have come back with you.

There is only one entrance and one exit to every crystal healing room, so you can't leave until your essence is back to its purest form. This is another process that can take varying lengths of time, depending on the nature and depth of the negativity you encountered in life. Once your normal vibrational energy has been restored, or you could say when your chakras have been realigned, you are ready to move on to the next step, the life review.

You can't enter your life review if you are still holding on to any negativity because that will prevent you from being impartial and dispassionate about the earth life you just finished. The learning process depends on being able to stand outside that life and see it as an observer, without attaching emotion to anything you see. And as we know, learning and growing from all that we do in our lives is the point of the whole exercise. Let's move on to an explanation of how the whole life review thing works.

8

Here Come da Judge

I had read and learned about the postgame life review before, and I always thought this was what people who had NDEs were referring to when they said that they saw their life flash before their eyes. Now I know that phenomenon occurs in the light tunnel, before you cross over to the other side. The real life review is much more detailed than anything that could flash before your eyes in a brief time.

The review begins in earnest after all the reacclimation necessary for the returning soul to feel at home again has been accomplished, as we talked about in the last chapter. Then all that person's guides have sort of an "Avengers assemble" moment in what looks very much like a situation room.

There are big viewing screens on the walls, and every minute detail of the life just lived will be observed on them. Sound like a squirm-inducing moment? It sort of does to me, but remember, there is no negativity involved in the process. It is a completely academic look, without emotion or judgment, at everything learned in that life. There is a listing of some of the learning opportunities that were missed and may need to be repeated in planning for the next life. In my case, Jasper can't keep himself from judging a little bit. But that's just the way he is, so the rest of us ignore it.

The guide that holds the original copy of your life plan, in my case his name is Joe, takes over as sort of the chairperson and directs what all the members of your team will be viewing on the screens. Since that particular guide holds the checklist of all the things you hoped to accomplish and learn with him at all times, he puts it on one of the screens and begins to check off what you did and didn't actually learn, whether you dealt with the negativity you prescribed for yourself or just sidestepped it, and if there are things from any and all your past lives that you wanted to conquer in the life you just lived but once again didn't.

For me, I have dragged a lot of emotional baggage with me through my many lives. But the one I think I may have finally at least put a dent in learning to manage is the one where I feel responsible for everybody and everything, which inevitably leads to feelings of victimhood and then to the one feeling we humans are in love with—personal martyrdom.

For some reason, maybe it's a reaction to the extremely negative atmosphere of earth, when we're incarnated, a lot of us love to assume that long-suffering martyr role. If it's not you, it's someone you know or are related to. We may hate to admit it, but it's usually the face in the mirror, the poor soul who is always the one left to clean up everybody else's messes. But that's okay, I don't mind, I'll take care of it. You go ahead and have a good time; I'll stay here. Sound familiar? Somehow, our puny human minds can twist that scenario into making us believe it's a noble thing to always play the victim when it's just stupidity. Nobody is the victim in their own lives. You choose the life you're living to learn what you wanted to learn. So learn it and move on.

Was I just up on a soapbox again? Sorry. Back to the life review.

Always remember that in spite of the title of this chapter, no one is going to judge you on how you performed in the life you just lived. Judging can be an extremely negative emotion, and it can't be said strongly or often enough that there is absolutely no negativity on the other side, only the positive, unconditional love of the Creator.

While the color red can denote anger in this dimension, red at home is just a beautiful color. White is not empty; it's all the colors together. Black is not dark and evil; it's just the opposite of white. The negative values that we place on almost everything while on earth have no validity on the other side, so our life review will have absolutely no assigning of right and wrong, or good and bad.

Like all the steps that must be taken when we return home after an earth life and before we can resume our real lives, the life review can take what would be a fair amount of earth time. Every minute detail of the life just lived is reviewed on the screens by the returning soul and all of his or her guides. What was learned will be checked off the list, and what wasn't will be examined and then will probably be forwarded to the next life for another try.

As an example, since the subject is death, did you live through the death of a loved one and develop the coping skills to be able to deal with your grief? If not, that learning process goes on the list for next time. In that way, it could be said that planning for your next life begins shortly after you arrive home from the one you just lived. But we'll leave that for future discussion.

The whole purpose of the life review is to gain clarity and understanding of the things we managed to learn while we were incarnated and to feel a complete sense of forgiveness for ourselves and for the things we didn't accomplish. And since we still have a little bit of humanness in there, for "bad" things we did and others did to us. We always have free choice and free will, whether incarnated or not, but nearly all the "bad" things that happen here on earth are planned before we incarnate, so forgiveness for those things really isn't necessary.

After everything has been reviewed and discussed by you and your guides, you have a team meeting with all your guides and any planners who might be helping you for a general discussion of what was learned, what wasn't, and what will be reused or set aside for next time. Then the minutes of that meeting are published, sort of like publishing a book. The information will be released for those on the other side to use in planning their own next incarnations. I guess you could say the synopses of all lives lived go into a sort of celestial cloud storage. I wonder if they use real clouds?

Once again, the life review is one of those things that takes as long as it takes. Since time as we know it doesn't exist on the other side, it's impossible to put constraints on it. Once it's complete, we proceed to what sounds to me to be one of the best steps in the whole process—the resting.

9

After Removing from the Oven, Let the Meat Rest

Almost anything you can think of in the physical world—from cells dividing to a roast or cake you just took out of the oven to your average toddler—has to have a resting phase. The same holds true for all of us who incarnate for lives on this planet after returning home to the other side.

During the life review that I described in the previous chapter, we dumped all the negativity that we picked up from our just-lived earth lives. Now, being surrounded by the positive, unconditional love of the Creator, we feel ready to take on the world again.

But just like that big turkey you pull out of the oven on Thanksgiving, we need a resting period to give us time to let our creative juices redistribute and settle. Our resting period takes place in a different area of home than the big, central square where all the shipping and receiving goes on. Since we still have a little bit of reacclimating to do, the area we go to will be a great deal like whatever part of the earth we just returned from. Even though we don't need them at home, there are houses and apartments that we will recognize as familiar and comfortable.

This area has also what I would describe as a long gallery with viewing screens that allow for observing the people you left behind to finish out their lives. But more about that later. There are also hundreds and hundreds of rooms where you can lower your vibration enough that you can make brief contact with your still incarnated love ones.

The guides say most people don't stay in this area very long because frankly, it gets boring, and most of the loved ones you're trying to contact choose not to see or hear you. Once you've decided you've spent enough time in this area, and only you can decide how long that will be, there are several choices you can make about moving forward.

First, you may be ready to resume your real life at home. I didn't get a lot of detail about what that would entail from the guides. They simply said that everyone has a job somewhere in the universe and that there are too many to mention. To provide a few examples that I am aware of, I, and people like me, help people in planning for their next incarnations. Barb and people like her help with the healing and cocooning of souls returning from earth incarnation. Many others act as teachers and advisers for people planning something special during their incarnations, like great talent in one area or another.

One thing I am absolutely sure of is that no one is floating around on a cloud and strumming a harp while singing hymns of praise. What an unbelievably boring way to spend eternity that would be!

As I said, I know the jobs Barb and I have at home. Barb continues her role as a healer, helping newly returned souls to detox and reacclimate. My job is helping people plan their next incarnations by using all the information collected in that cloud from all the lives anyone in the universe ever lived. Another friend of Barb's, Renée, helps people prepare for the physical transition back into an earthly incarnation.

I think it's safe to say that all jobs on the other side involve learning of some kind, whether it be all those engaged in helping with incarnation, which would include all the spirit guides, or some kind of research and experimentation to help solve our problems here on earth. I do know that all scientific and cultural advancements seen in this dimension are first created on the other side and then either brought here with someone when they are born or transmitted to them while they are working on that particular problem during their earth lives. In either case, everything is planned well in advance.

If you don't want to immediately go back to "work "after transitioning and reacclimating, there are a couple of other options. One of them that the guides told Barb and me about is something we decided to term a "void" life.

A void life is not really a life as we would define it on earth. It's a period (even though there is no such thing as time at home) that might better be described as what in the 1960s and 1970s was called sensory deprivation. Back in those ancient times, people floated naked in a tank of warm saltwater that was in a darkened and soundproof enclosure for an indeterminate amount of time.

It was supposed to let you completely clear your mind and connect with your higher consciousness. Did it work? I never knew anybody who tried it, and the fact that it's no longer popular speaks to how well it worked, I think. There was also a horror movie about someone who turned into an evolutionary monster while in sensory deprivation, so that probably didn't do much to help make it more than a fad.

The void life involves the soul entering a velvety black area that is completely free of any type of emotion, except for the unconditional love of the Creator. In this space, you feel like you're being cradled in a soft blanket, much like the cocooning that may occur soon after our initial transition. The difference is cocooning is a necessary part of helping us get reaccustomed to the other side, while the void life is a lot like taking a refreshing and much-needed nap, which is the point of the whole exercise.

When you decide to leave this space, you feel relaxed, recharged, and ready to move forward. Believe me, when Barb and I were allowed to experience this place for even the short amount of time we were there, we felt like we never wanted it to end.

Another type of interim life Barb and I were told about was an "ascension" life. This is sort of the yin to the yang of the void life because instead of being swaddled in a comforting darkness, you are constantly bathed in the beautiful white light created by the unconditional love of the Creator. Again, it is a life completely void of any emotion other than love. The similarities between these lives are that like everything at home, you choose which you want and for how long you want to experience either of them. You only emerge when you feel you're ready to resume your regular life.

Many souls who choose either of these lives have returned from a life of extreme hardship, either physical or mental, and need a little extra help to get back in balance by releasing any pieces of retained negativity.

After going through any or all the above steps that you need and want to, and getting your vibrational energy level recalibrated so you are fully functional at home again, you approach a point where you can make one of several decisions. All are yours to make using your free will. First, you can choose to stay at home and work at whatever research and learning you love to do. Imagine having a job you love to do! Or you may choose to experience a life on another planet or in another dimension just to see what that would be like. Or you may want to go on what I would consider the ultimate in getting away from it all, the "just be" life.

Neither Barb nor I could come up with a more descriptive term than "just be," so we decided to go with it. Here again, what I'm about to tell you may cause you to think, *This guy is way nuts,* but I'm telling it to you the way it was related to us. You may find yourself saying, just like Jerry said to Elaine, "How can it be?" My answer, of course, just like Elaine's, is, "Oh, it be."

The just be life takes place when you reduce yourself to your purest essence and then organically join with an organism or inanimate object, either in the earth dimension or in another dimension, and for a time, just be. You may be part of a rock, a tree, an ocean, or the atmosphere, but whatever you choose, you are just a part of a much larger whole.

You have absolutely no responsibilities other than to be what you are, the purest essence of you. While neither Barb nor I have been allowed to see ourselves in this type of life, I have no doubt that we have lived it at some point. It is the ultimate recharge of the old batteries and allows you to feel the ultimate in interconnectedness that we give up when we incarnate as humans.

In fact, much of the negative energy that surrounds us here on earth is created by our feelings of subconscious anger about the fact we can never really feel the interconnectedness we have all the time at home. We're like the people who put on those sumo wrestler suits and bounce off each other, never able to make real contact. We join clubs, churches, political parties, or any other type of group to feel as connected as we do at home. But it just isn't possible to feel it to the same degree while we inhabit these human bodies.

And as we, as a species, become more and more urbanized and disconnected from each other, the frustration grows larger and larger. The problem is that we have created this problem, and we are the only ones who can fix it. We just don't want to look up from our phones long enough to try. We might miss a Facebook post.

I am old enough to remember when people used to go to each other's homes just to visit, talk, and reconnect. Now, we all just text each other, so there isn't even a voice connection anymore. The only upside I can see for all our modern-day lack of feeling truly connected with other people is that it can lead to feeling a need to become more spiritual and introspective to feel more connected to the universe and/or whatever you envision God to be.

We all know people who just love going to the beach or the mountains and being close to nature. The reason behind those cravings, if I can call them that, is that in all the areas of the planet that have not been paved over and built on, the essence of souls in their just be lives are present, and our subconscious minds can feel that essence in a walk along the beach or a hike through the woods. When we subconsciously sense that connection to the universe and know it is there, we want more of that feeling of being connected. We want to be reminded on a soul level that we are more than the physical body we inhabit, and when we return home to the other side, we can feel reconnected to every other part of the universe again. Be a tree hugger? Hell yeah. If it makes you feel good, why not?

I guess to summarize the different types of lives I just listed, I would say they are all different types of vacations, exactly like the ones we take during our earth incarnations. We work, work, work, take our two weeks to do something fun and different to get rested and recharged to be able to go back to work, work, work some more until our next vacation. In our real lives on the other side, we incarnate, live a life, go home, take a break, start planning for our next incarnation, incarnate, and repeat the cycle. Which, coincidentally, brings us to our next topic, which is how we go about planning our next incarnation.

10
Home and Dry

I've made a lot of references to Jasper in my writing, and as you know by now, he is my main spirit guide. He has become, in the relatively short time I've been consciously aware of his presence in my life, someone I listen to and trust to tell me the unvarnished truth. He also occupies the role of my educator about the nature of the universe and how it functions. In short, I am him, and he is me. And because of that, his help is invaluable as I try to move ever forward in my spiritual journey.

One of the things that has been sorely lacking in this book so far has been my customary references to pop culture and old movies and TV shows, and believe me, that fact has not gone unnoticed by Jasper. He has been quiet as a mouse lately, not only because he is bored to tears with the subject of death because it doesn't exist for him, but also because he has rarely been mentioned, and we're already up to chapter 10!

Part of the problem with the lack of participation by Jasper is that his original idea for the title of this book was something like "The Giant Roller Coaster of Death." His premise was that souls are enticed to keep reincarnating on this planet because of the weird way, in universal terms, that we treat the death of our physical bodies. With all that is attached to that, it's like being on an emotional roller coaster. So being the adrenaline junkies that we all are, we come here like we flock to Disney World for the thrill ride of experiencing death.

I get what he wanted us to understand, sort of, but a more adult theme was chosen. So now he's going to pout the whole time I'm writing this. But really, Jasper, let's face it, death is not something most people find to be a laugh a minute subject, so the whole tone of this book has been more serious than I usually am or like to be. Maybe now that we've gotten the death stuff behind us and can focus on the life stuff, I can lighten things up a little.

Starting with the title of this chapter. "Home and Dry" is the name of a song recorded by Gerry Rafferty in 1978. It references a term mostly used in Britain that means you accomplished what you set out to do, and you are where you want to be. That is the feeling we all have after living out our earthly incarnation, returning home, detoxing, and downloading everything we learned.

We're all home and dry, living our real lives on the other side. Then we start to feel a little tug, then a pull, then an outright calling to go back and do it all again. It's like being in a meeting at work but knowing there is chocolate cake in the break room. Pretty soon, all you can focus on is how good that cake will taste, and you can't wait for the meeting to be over so you can have a slice. Or two.

There is a difference, however. When your meeting at work is over, you can make a dash for the break room and pounce on the cake. But when you succumb to the lure of reincarnating, you can't just fling yourself into it. It requires a great deal of preparation and planning. That is what we talk about in the next chapter.

Before we get into that topic in detail, I think we need to discuss the one thing that is not only the glue that holds the universe together but the lubricant that makes it all run smoothly. That thing is unconditional love.

A lot has been and continues to be written about the concept of unconditional love, whether it be concerning love of self or others. But it is such a nebulous and emotion-packed term that people have a hard time wrapping their heads and arms around it.

When we are at home on the other side, we are surrounded and bathed in the unconditional love of the Creator and the other energies there at all times. However, when we incarnate on this planet, we become surrounded by the negativity that is pervasive here, so it's sometimes difficult to remember what unconditional love feels like. It's even more difficult to pull it out of the atmosphere and back into our daily lives.

I know the word *negative* usually has a bad connotation, but experiencing the negativity on this planet is why we come to live out earthly lives here. So instead of thinking of negativity as a bad thing, consider it as just another kind of energy. After all, every battery has a positive and a negative end, and without the two working together, no power can be produced.

So instead of looking at negativity as something bad or evil, remove the human emotion from it, and see it as a necessary counterbalance to the positive side of all energy. If you don't have the negatives in your life, you don't have the power you need to move toward more positivity. In other words, you must know what you don't want in your life before you can be clear about what you do want.

At a recent session I had with Barb, Jasper appeared as Jim Phelps, listening to the tape recorder (you're going to have to google that one, young people) that appeared at the beginning of every episode of the original *Mission: Impossible* TV series in the 1960s (another google, young friends). Jasper told me my mission, should I choose to accept it (like I have a choice), is to explain the concept of unconditional love in terms average people can understand and obtain the clarity of understanding that allows them to make unconditional love of themselves and others a permanent part of their everyday lives.

That is the key to unlocking the door to a future that contains everything everybody wants for themselves and others. Then he went into a whole Alice in Wonderland thing about that same key providing entrance to a world where anything and everything is possible. But I think we'll save that whole story for another time. He's a little disappointed because he had at least ten wardrobe changes planned for that whole experience, but it can wait.

My first thought was the same as when he told me I needed to come up with a new word to replace the word, *death*. I said, sure, how hard can that be? Completely changing the way people think about loving themselves and others-won't take more than an hour or two, surely. *Au contraire*, Mr. J., this is going to take some time and effort, and don't call me Shirley. I'm willing to put in that time and effort, however, because I think it is essential to all spiritual growth to understand unconditional love. So let's push on.

Unconditional love is such a difficult thing for us to understand when we're incarnated here because the majority of us have rarely seen or experienced it. Perhaps more important, we have such deep-seated and closely held feelings about what it might be that, even if we intellectually know what we think it is, we are pretty sure we couldn't possibly deserve it. The closest any of us may have come to experiencing unconditional love is if we have or interact with pets.

Pets, for the most part, love their humans unconditionally. Dogs will be there for you no matter what kind of mood you're in. Every time they see you, it's like they fall in love all over again, and even when humans are abusive to them, they still want to love them. There may be the occasional pooping in a shoe, but that's more likely a commentary on a current minor problem than an overall lack of love. I know more than a few humans who would much rather have pets in their lives than humans because there is very little risk that your animal is not going to love you back.

It makes perfect sense to those people to avoid the chance of being hurt by not having your affections reciprocated by someone you care about. But in doing that, they are missing the entire point of why we come here in the first place. Like they say in the lottery commercials, you gotta play to win! It is very rare to find love without experiencing some hurt along the way. Remember when I said you have to know what you don't want before you can know what you do want? That's how we learn to cope with the hurt and by coping, grow spiritually.

I believe the part of understanding unconditional love that we all have the most trouble with is the actual meaning of the word *unconditional.* It simply means without any conditions attached. When we're in our human state, it's nearly impossible for us to grasp that basic concept because all the love we've had from the day we were born has had any number of conditions attached to it.

Those of us who grew up in organized religion were always taught to believe that God loved us unconditionally but only if we believed certain things, performed certain rituals, or, most especially, showed up at church every Sunday with that offering envelope. None of that is unconditional love; that is love with tons of conditions attached. Organized religion tells us we are only worthy of God's unconditional love if we do this or that or don't do the other thing, which it decided to call "sins."

The word "sin" is derived from an ancient Greek word that simply means missing the mark, as in not hitting the bull's-eye in archery. If you prefer, sin could also be derived from ancient Hebrew (more biblical, after all), where again it meant to be absent or missing. It wasn't until the early Christian era, when the church was looking for ways to scare people into believing in the new church dogma, that sins started to be spelled out and defined as one-way tickets to hell, which was another church-invented control measure.

Just as important, the church used the many sins it had decided we all are guilty of as the things we absolutely had to stop doing to deserve God's love. But since they bought in to the story of

Eve and the apple, we all were born in terrible sin, so we could never really be worthy.

To this day, one of organized religion's favorite sayings is, "All have fallen short of the glory of God." Because they have tried to attach so many conditions to that glory, that unconditional love, it seems to be impossible for anyone trying to live a normal earth life to attain it. This is one of the more egregious ways that organized religion blocks people from spiritual growth.

I recently saw a young man with a tattoo on his arm that read, "Fear God." If anything drives me crazy (and a lot of people would say that's not a drive; it's a short walk), it's this idea that we should be afraid of God. If our understanding of unconditional love was clearer and not purposefully confused by thousands of years of the teachings of organized religion, we would know there is absolutely no reason to fear a being who not only loves us unconditionally but is entirely composed of nothing but unconditional love.

I believe there are three phases of unconditional love, with one phase cascading into the next. The first phase is the unconditional love that the Creator has for us in an unending supply. The second phase is the unconditional love we should have for ourselves, which is a continuation and reflection of the unconditional love the Creator has for us. And third, last but certainly not least, is the unconditional love we have for those around us.

Since I think we struggle most with the second phase of unconditional love, let's examine that one first.

The problems we have with understanding the second phase starts practically the day we're born through the interactions between us and our parents and immediate family. Many young children start to lose that feeling of being unconditionally loved when their parents start to withhold love as a means of getting the child to behave as they want them to. The children feel they only receive love, and are only deserving of love, when they clean their rooms or finish all the food on their plates. As they get older, they are only loved if they get good grades or make the football team or cheerleading squad.

Once they start to develop relationships outside the immediate family, they start thinking that no one will love them unless they look, dress, or act a certain way. Because we experienced this placing of conditions on the love we receive from all the important people surrounding us as our young lives developed, we start to lose the feeling of unconditional love for ourselves. We come to think we don't deserve it. Once that feeling sets in, it's nearly impossible for us to feel unconditional love for anyone else, which leads to an inability to form lasting relationships.

According to a recent article in the *Huffington Post*, the US divorce rate has dropped from a high of 51 percent to around 40 percent, but that is still a big number, and it didn't come out of nowhere. It came from people trying to find unconditional love outside themselves before they have it inside. It's like trying to create positive energy from a battery that only has two negative poles. It can't be done.

Even though being loved and feeling the love of those around us in our earth lives is important to our emotional well-being, that feeling of unconditional love for ourselves is even more important. After all, we can't truly share something we don't have. The problem lies in the earthly reality that not only are very few of us taught to love ourselves unconditionally, we are often taught it is a bad thing to love ourselves at all. It's regarded as being egotistical or too self-involved if you actually admit to someone that you love yourself.

I've written before that one of my mother's favorite little phrases when I was growing up was, "Self-praise stinks," which she threw at me whenever I was feeling good about some little thing I accomplished at school. The saying was a direct descendant of that good, old, Protestant puritan mainstay, "Pride goeth before a fall."

Whichever way you choose to phrase it, what she was teaching me was that it was never okay to tell yourself you did a good job or feel good about yourself for any reason. Is it any wonder that for much of my adult life, I barely liked myself, let alone loved myself unconditionally? I know there are many, many people out there who felt, and still feel, the same way.

So how do we go about changing that program in our heads our subconscious mind loves to keep running; the one telling us we're not deserving or worthy of being loved? The first step, I think, is to know and trust that unconditional love actually exists and is available to us. We can start to do that by addressing unconditional love in the three phases I mentioned previously.

We've talked about the second phase, which is unconditional love of self, but before we can take on the third phase—unconditionally loving those around us and the world at large—there's some more work to be done on the second phase. This work involves removing all the anger, fear, and guilt we have accumulated over the course of a lifetime about what we feel we have done wrong. You can't possibly love yourself and have enough love to give others if you are going to cling to the anger you feel about how you have behaved and the guilt that accompanies it.

I wrote at length about conquering the three ugly stepsisters—fear, anger, and guilt—in my book *Clearing the Track,* so I'm not going to go into that issue in great depth here. Just as with all types of unconditional love, the important point to remember is that loving yourself unconditionally simply means loving yourself without condition.

That means you can't think about how you can't love yourself because of the way you talked to your grandmother or the way you treated your parents, husband, child, coworker, or whomever. First and foremast, you must stop whatever behavior makes you feel the anger and guilt and then forgive yourself.

Always remember that all our life experiences can and should be regarded as learning opportunities. Take the emotion out of the situation, and see it as a chance to learn compassion, patience, or tolerance, whatever it is you feel you should be learning and then move on. Once you give yourself the gift of unconditional love, it's a brand-new day.

Of course, there will be times when you backslide and don't feel the love because your subconscious wants to keep running all those old programs that say you aren't worthy of love. You know that old saying that your mother can push all your buttons because she is the one who installed most of them? When your mother isn't around, your subconscious is only too happy to take over and start punching the old buttons.

The problem is, being angry at yourself for any reason only makes your forward movement that much more difficult. So forgive yourself as many times as you have to in order to break that vicious cycle, especially if some of your guilt comes from a falling out you may have had with someone who has transitioned. Believe me, once we go home, all those negative human interactions are forgiven and forgotten. So don't waste time worrying that Mom and Dad are still mad about any disagreements you may have had when they were incarnated. They couldn't care less once they get home.

Understanding the first and second phases of unconditional love is essential to being able to use that love to accomplish the third phase. So let's go over that first phase one more time.

Understanding the first phase of unconditional love, that which comes to us from the Creator, brings a realization that almost everything you've been taught about the Creator of the universe being an angry, vengeful, punishing entity who will only love you if you follow a laundry list of rules laid down in the writings of the men of organized religion is just not true.

All those rules and regulations were put in place to advance the cause of organized religion and assert its complete control of the lives of its adherents. They have very little to do with encouraging spiritual growth. I know I often write about organized religion in a disparaging way, but the only real issues I have with that belief system are twofold. First, it holds itself out to be the gatekeeper to intimate contact with the Creator. In fact and practice, organized religion often just obstructs the path. Second, it insists the Creator is only there to judge and punish you.

Let me say it as often as I have to: unconditional love means love without condition. No strings attached. This means that no matter what you believe, think, or do, the Creator still loves you, even if you get to the point of believing there is no Creator! All conditions placed on receiving unconditional love from the universe were invented and placed there by the men who wrote the so-called holy books of the world for their own purposes, which usually were to control people and reinforce their own prejudices and desires. Can I be any clearer? I hope I can convince at least some of you of the truth of that last statement.

The third phase of unconditional love is to be able to give that love to other people. The first two phases of understanding of unconditional love absolutely must be accomplished and incorporated into your everyday life before you can even attempt to move to the third phase, which is giving that love away.

As the old saying goes, you can't drink from a well that's gone dry. You first must possess something before you can give it away. So let's assume you have laid that foundation of unconditional love for yourself and believe the Creator of the universe is composed of unconditional love and has nothing but unconditional love for you.

Once you have conquered the first two phases of understanding, you may find the third phase is pretty easy to do because you've increased your positive energy to a place where people with a like kind of energy are more attracted to you, making it easier to form relationships.

The three phases of unconditional love that I just described might be easier to visualize if you see them as a beautiful waterfall with three cascades, each flowing into the next. The first cascade comes from the source of the never-ending supply of unconditional love, the Creator of the universe. It flows into you and fills you up so that it can flow into the third cascade and into all the people around you. It's a beautiful waterfall that never stops flowing.

I've written before about the safety lecture given by flight attendants before every takeoff that we all tend to ignore. In it, for those of you that weren't ever listening, they tell you that if the oxygen masks drop from the overhead compartment, you should always put yours on first before you help others around you. I know the first instinct of many people, especially those traveling with children, would be to put the mask on them first. But if you pass out before you can do that, everybody dies.

I don't think it's an outlandish idea to compare unconditional love to oxygen. We need both to grow, survive, and thrive while we're in these physical bodies. It's easier for us to understand the concept of dying from a lack of oxygen than it is from a lack of love, but both are very real. Dying from a lack of love just takes longer. It even has a name, a medical condition called "failure to thrive," often seen in young children and the elderly. Nothing may be physically wrong with these individuals, but they literally waste away from lack of love and human interaction.

Though the focus of this chapter has been unconditional love and how it is vital to the successful living out of a life on this planet, the guides want us to be aware that love is not the only unconditional thing available to us from the other side. They have been using words like "acceptance," "trust," "support," "gratitude," and anything else that could be considered a positive energy. All are available unconditionally from the other side.

A very good way to understand the help that is available to us from home is to think back to your teenage years, if you can remember back that far. It would be a rare thing if your parents were unconditionally loving, supporting, accepting, and trusting you at that point in your life. More likely the complete opposite because as we all know, and would admit if we were being truthful with ourselves, we did some pretty reckless and stupid things when we were young. At least I did. Our parents tried to teach us by making all kinds of rules and regulations, which, of course, we did our best to ignore.

Anyone who has raised teenagers knows you can't really tell them anything because they already know everything. So who were our biggest supporters when we were that age? Our circle of friends.

Whether a large or small group, they were always there when we decided to do something stupid and would always answer, "I'm in," when asked if they wanted to join in the fun; no questions asked.

The analogy here is your guides and helpers on the other side. Because they love and support you unconditionally, they are more like the friends you had as a teenager than your parents. If you decide to go off track and do something stupid in your earth life, they may ask, "Are you sure?" But if your answer is, "Hell, yeah," they will be all in for whatever ride you want to go on, even if they know it's not exactly what you planned before you incarnated. If you decide to use your free will to go off script, they will unconditionally support you. Whatever the outcome, they will be there, acting from their unconditional love for you to help you get back on track.

The guides are saying that instead of enumerating all the many positive energies available to us from the other side to help us along the way, we can just call it access to the unconditional universe and the unconditional love that comes with it. None of us could make it through an incarnation on this planet without a lot of help from the other side, even if we don't know, feel, or acknowledge that it's there. Just be happy it is!

11

What's the Point?

Since this spiritual journey began for me in earnest about three years ago, Jasper and the rest of the guides have told me at length about how we choose the things we want to work on while we're incarnated on earth. Then they explained how we make a detailed life plan that will best help us accomplish our learning goals.

Because this book is a closer look at both death and life, the guides helping me write it have provided a lot more detail about how we go about planning our earth lives. I'm happy to share that information here.

But before we get into all that. Let's think about that age-old and largely unanswered question, what is the meaning of life? Why do we do this? More important, since we know we plan our own lives, why do we do this to ourselves?

Of course, organized religion will tell you that we are here to suffer and be miserable. I grudgingly acknowledge that is partially true, just not for the reasons they want you to think. If we suffer and are miserable, it's because we choose to do that for our own learning, not because we are being punished for imaginary sins. Religious dogma would have you buy into the whole Adam and Eve thing, which means every human born on the planet is coated in original sin, accomplishing two things that greatly benefit organized religion and its financial status.

First, because Eve brought sin into the world, it allows for the denigration of women as a whole. Second, it allows for the subjugation of all humans because only organized religion holds the secret to cleansing people of sin, at least enough to be judged by some God sitting on a throne somewhere. Think that might be a little too harsh of an assessment of the state of organized religion? Sorry, but I don't.

I was raised in a mainline Protestant denomination and taught to believe all the things I was supposed to, no matter how illogical they were. But as I grew older and became more aware of the true nature of spirituality, I felt that belonging to a specific church didn't really matter that much, and going to church every Sunday just for appearances' sake became less and less important.

And now, as organized religion in the United States becomes increasingly fundamentalist in an attempt to hold on to its donation-giving members, I'm happier than ever that I walked away. Organized religion has replaced true spirituality with a near hysteria over social issues. Bible stories are cherry-picked for quotes that justify bigotry and hatred of all kinds. People who were commanded to "judge not lest ye be judged" are falling over themselves in a rush to judge other people on how they live, how they look, or what they believe.

But all these things aside, the reason organized religion as we know it is going the way of the dinosaur is because, like everything regressive in this world, it blocks people's access to true spirituality instead of enhancing it as it should be doing.

Let me just say I am a survivor who walked away from all the dogma religion has in place to constrain spiritual growth. I've never felt more connected to my spiritual side, and I feel more connected to it every day.

Let's get back to the fundamentals of life planning by returning to the question of why we do it all. First and foremost, as I've written before, all the souls who make the decision to incarnate on this planet are adrenaline junkies. We could choose to spend eternity safely at home, learning from everyone else's life experiences. But like the Dauntless faction from the book and movie *Divergent*, we see that train with the open doors coming down the track and can't stop ourselves from jumping on and seeing where the ride will take us.

For those of us who grew up in rural areas, a good analogy for the whole process might be a comparison with cow tipping. If you didn't have the good fortune (?) of growing up in the country, let me explain the whole phenomenon of cow tipping.

At night, in the summertime, cows sometimes stay out in the fields instead of going into the barn. While most of them lie down to sleep, a couple usually stand because, like horses, they can lock their knees in place when they are asleep. The object of the exercise is to sneak up on the ones that are standing and push them over, thus accomplishing cow tipping. Did I mention there are varying amounts of alcohol consumption required before anyone undertakes this? And that usually the one who consumes the most alcohol insists on being the "tipper"?

Let me say here, I disavow any personal participation in this incredibly stupid game, but I happen to know the fine points.

First, cows are not as tame and docile as you think, so they're a little tough to sneak up on, especially when approached by several people laughing, giggling, and sliding around in cow pies. Second, cows are not small. They weigh fifteen hundred or sixteen hundred pounds, and since they are standing on four legs, they are not easy to tip. And third, cows, for some reason, don't enjoy being tipped over, so even if you manage to do it, they go down kicking and snorting. Kids, don't try this at home.

How does cow tipping in any way relate to choosing to incarnate for another life on this planet? Believe it or not, the processes are the same. We are living at home, intoxicated with being in an environment with no negativity and constantly surrounded by the unconditional love of the Creator. Then we and a couple of the souls who will be our guides decide it would be fun to do something different, albeit stupid and dangerous. So you plan to go to a farm (earth), find a cow, (life), and see if you can tip it over, knowing full well that it might kick the living daylights out of you on its way down. Your friends (guides) will stand back, watch, and offer advice and encouragement. And after you experience the whole thing, everybody runs home, and you talk about what happened for days. Then, of course, you have to share the adventure with the whole world because it's just too good a story to keep to yourself.

Still questioning why it is we choose to live an earth life after that great story? I can understand completely. Jasper has told me several times that the more you grow to understand how the universe works, the less black and white things become.

When we are incarnated here on earth, we don't like gray areas. We want everything to be good or bad. But in universal reality, everything is relative, and things are rarely as we assume them to be. So looking at an earth life from the perspective of the other side, we don't see anything as being a good or bad experience. Everything is just an experience, so why not try it?

Let's go back to one of the original premises the guides use to teach us about the nature of life on earth. That is the comparison of incarnation to video games. Being of a certain age, I preferred the old-school games like Space Invaders or even Frogger. In those games, you start out at the lowest point, work your way up the various levels by learning how to play the game, accumulate points (knowledge) along the way, and eventually either win and exit the game, or get killed and then get as many more lives as you want or need to accomplish your learning goals.

Bottom line, no matter what else is involved, it's all about learning and growing spiritually from what you learn. Think of it this way. Let's say you want to learn patience, which is one of the things I know I've been working on in this life and several others. Because earthly linear time doesn't exist on the other side, there is no need for anyone to be patient. There are no lines and no waiting for anything, so a lot of people choose to examine how patience works during their earthly lives because it is an unknown emotion at home. And we all know some people who are much further along in learning patience than others.

But at home during life planning, you decide to pick patience from the list of available character traits as one of the things you want to thoroughly understand and incorporate into your essence. Since this is the first time you are choosing patience, when you put it on your list, it's printed in plain block letters, much like a first-grader would print it. As you work on developing patience in your earth lives, and as you grow to understand what it means, the word *patience* on your list will change and be written in cursive. As you learn more about being patient with each successive life you live and incorporate it into your daily earth life, more and more embellishments are added to the word *patience* on your list.

It may take several lives to really learn the meaning of patience and have a complete understanding that makes it a part of who you are. Once that happens, "patience" will be written in beautiful calligraphy on your list. With complete understanding, that handsome written word can be coated in gold, removed from your list, and hung on your wall at home, just like you can hang all your degrees and diplomas on your office wall here on earth.

That's how living on earth life relates to our learning to accomplish the growth of our souls. Each time we can gain a full understanding of any positive attribute and incorporate it into the essence of who we are, it's like getting another diploma that proves we completed the course of learning and have mastered the subject.

You might ask at this point, if our real lives on the other side are lived surrounded only by the unconditional love of the Creator and in an atmosphere completely free of negativity, don't we already have all these diplomas on the wall? No, not really. Because we are in that positive environment, all the understanding there comes not from direct experience but from learning about the experiences of others. So it's not really an earned understanding.

As another example, let's say you are fascinated by the history of the Roman Empire, like I am, so you become a history major in college, get your BS, MS, and PhD all in Roman history, read everything that was written about Rome, know every little factoid available about the thousand years of Roman history from the founding of the Republic to the fall of the Empire, but you never leave your hometown.

You've never gone to Rome to walk through the ruins of the Forum. Never visited Pompeii, Hadrian's Wall, or any other place around the Mediterranean where vestiges of the Empire still exist. You know everything there is to know about the Roman Empire, yet there are still big gaps in your understanding because you haven't seen or touched any piece of ancient Rome that still is there. You've never been on a field trip to complete your education.

Field trip is the phrase the guides have asked me to use to describe incarnating for a life on earth. Even though we have access to all the information in the universe when we are at home, including the accounts of every life that was ever lived by every soul who has incarnated on earth, reading and learning about something without experiencing it can never take the place of the field trip. Through a field trip, you and your senses can touch, see, hear, and maybe even smell and taste whatever it is you are trying to learn.

While no one at home is ever judged for not wanting to incarnate and live out an earth life, those who don't have to gain an understanding of it by reading about the experiences of those of us who do. Without that field trip, the understanding can never be as total and complete. That's why the incarnators get those golden words to hang on the wall, to enhance the feeling of accomplishment. All done without the negative emotions of gloating and jealousy, I might add.

I feel I might be getting close to belaboring the issue of why we do all of this, but I've had these questions in my mind, so I know other people have them also. I hope the guides have brought some clarity to the issue for all of us. If all those explanations still seem kind of vague or nebulous, I understand. The guides say that answering the question of why has been the hardest thing for our puny human minds to grasp.

If nothing else works for you, consider why people climb Mount Everest, run marathons, or do anything that seems impossibly dangerous. Because it's there. Because they can. We incarnate as humans on this planet and put ourselves through all these life scenarios because we can, and because we crave that feeling of accomplishment that comes after.

Out of all the lifeforms on all the planets in all the galaxies, we who incarnate on this small planet filled with negativity are the ones who can say, "Yes, I did, and I am a more contented soul for doing it." "Steel burnished by fire," as the old saying goes.

Above all else, the guides want us to always remember that this whole experience is nothing more than a game we all play, and we tend to take it way too seriously when we're here. It's supposed to be fun, even when it seems the world is falling apart around you. It may help to always bear in mind that your real life is only lived at home on the other side, so no matter what you must endure while you are incarnated, it's not real and can never alter our sacred inner self.

Great actors can play many roles convincingly, but who they really are never changes. Tom Hanks has portrayed dozens of people in dozens of scenarios. But when the movie wraps production and he goes home, he is still Tom Hanks. It's the same for all of us.

I think it's now time to move on to the nuts and bolts of the planning process we go through before each of our incarnations.

12

Fail to Plan, Plan to Fail 2.0

I think, and I hope, we got some of our "why" questions answered in the last chapter. So let's move on to answering some of our "how" questions.

After you've lived your earth life, transitioned home, detoxed, debriefed, rested and relaxed, perhaps even traveled, for as long as you need and want, you may decide you would like to incarnate for a life on earth thing all over again. This is the point where the work that precedes the real work of living a life on earth begins.

We learned that during our time in the crystal room, when we are being detoxed from the negativity we brought back from earth with us. Those pieces of negative emotions that are removed from the essence of who we really are become part of a list kept for us to remind us of the things we might want to work on resolving in future incarnations. The guides say this is what karma truly is: the things you haven't resolved in an earth life that you want to at least work on resolving in your next life.

People think karma means that what goes around, comes around, and the negative things that happen to you in this life are a result of negative things you did to others in a past life. The problem with that way of looking at karma is that it implies that somewhere, someone or something is judging you and then punishing you for things you did that it doesn't like, which is never the case.

You plan whatever happens to you during your earth life—positive or negative—for the learning experience it gives you. The experience also helps in developing coping mechanisms to deal with life scenarios you can't experience while immersed in the atmosphere of unconditional love at home.

This is the reason that a list is made and kept for you after detox. Just as we have amnesia about being in the totally positive atmosphere of the other side when we incarnate on earth, we tend to develop selective amnesia about all the negativity we encountered during our earth lives. It's just like women having babies. If they remember how painful it was, they would never have another one. So they get a little amnestic about the bad parts.

It's safe to say that the initial planning for a future earth incarnation begins when we transition home and our karma list is made for us by the people helping us detox. All that negativity must be removed from our essences before our life reviews begin, so we can be impartial about what we are see and how we cope with the life scenarios we put ourselves through. The karma list will be saved and put on our cosmic to-do list by our guides.

With the clarity and understanding we gained from reviewing our most recent earth lives with our guides, and with our karma lists always at hand, we start to decide if we will revisit things we didn't get a diploma for this time around. Or perhaps set them aside and work on something entirely different. We always have free will to decide what we want to do and advice from our guides to help us make those decisions.

Jasper says about 90 percent of the time during the initial meeting I have with him and my other guides after we decide to come back for another life, I ignore the advice of everyone assembled because I have a real, "Been there, done that," kind of attitude. This always leads to a DISCUSSION (all caps according to him) among all of us.

But since I am the one doing the incarnating, I always win that argument. The caveat here is that just because you choose not to keep working on a particular theme or scenario doesn't mean it goes away. That's the purpose of the karma list. It's a permanent reminder of the things you started but didn't finish. At some point, you will have to work on them all to get that diploma and graduate.

Before we get into the actual planning of lives and the cool computer screens we use for that, let's talk about time. When the guides tell Barb and I about some process we all go through in transitioning home from our lives or planning for our next ones, they say it will take a certain number of hours, days, or weeks in earth time. According to Jasper, when we incarnate, we become obsessed with knowing how long things take.

For the most part, I just disregard that information. First, I don't think it's that important to know it can take up to thirty-five hundred hours to plan an earth life. And second, I think our friends on the other side really suck at interpreting earth time. They just have no frame of reference, so things they tell us will occur may happen tomorrow, next week, or next year, depending on when things in a chain of events are supposed to occur first take place. So it's not that they are unreliable in what they tell us; they are incapable of lying or deceiving. They are just giving a best-guess estimate, and it is not always as accurate as we would like it to be.

One thing about time that I do think they understand is the amount of it that elapses between earth lives. Depending on the specific type of earth life you choose, it can be seventy-five to a hundred years between lives. For some people, it can be five hundred or more years. And for others, incarnating can be a once and done kind of thing. It is a freewill choice made entirely by the soul incarnating.

After choosing the time frame for our next incarnation, we can then choose between basically two different kinds of lives. The first I call, for lack of a better term, an “academic life.” I chose this term because this life is about helping other souls to learn something. This kind of life is usually short and choppy, often ending in an early “death,” sometimes in a traumatic way. We choose this life to help other souls with their soul growth while learning something for ourselves without becoming enmeshed in an entire lifelong scenario. The prime example here would be a parent losing a child. The child would be living a short academic life as a way to help the souls incarnated as his or her parents develop the emotional skills necessary to cope with the loss of a child.

The person living the academic life will often have one of the souls who assumed the parent role take on an academic life for him or her next time around to start developing the same coping skills for dealing with that particularly painful sense of loss.

The other thing you can do in an academic life is sort of audition some emotional scenario that you're not too sure you want to deal with or focus on for an entire life. A good example of this are children and young people who participate in physical abuse and/or a murder scenario. You are trying out the experience to see if you want to develop the coping skills people who suffer years of abuse and neglect come to learn.

You may also choose an academic life just to deliver a specific message or provide some kind of an example. Not many souls who choose academic lives become famous, but Mattie Stepanek would be a good example of that kind of academic life. Mattie was born with a rare type of muscular dystrophy that confined him to a wheelchair at an early age and eventually caused him to need breathing support. At the age of three, he wrote his first poems. He went on to write seven best-selling books of poetry, including the famous *Heartsongs* when he was eleven.

Mattie transitioned at the age of thirteen. But in his short time here on earth, he had friends and admirers as diverse as Oprah Winfrey and President Jimmy Carter, and he inspired many others with his writings. It takes a very strong soul to be able to choose a life like Mattie lived, but while he and his loved ones were learning coping skills pertaining to his life and death, he was teaching all of us about life and love.

Most of us know or have known of people who had children transition at a young age, so choosing an academic life is not that uncommon. That kind of life brings huge opportunities for growth through learning for all the parties involved, even those outside the immediate family.

In this age of social media, the financial or emotional needs of a child with a very serious illness are often posted online by someone close to the situation. As a result, people all over the world respond with money, get well cards, or just plain old thoughts and prayers. It's a drawing together—either informally or in an organized fashion, like the Children's Miracle Network—souls feel good about participating in because it provides a familiar vibration of the interconnectedness of everything in the universe, both here and on the other side.

The other type of life we can choose, the one we choose more often, I call a "web life" because you are connected to any number of other souls at the various stages of your life. This type of life requires a great deal more planning and coordination than an academic life because based on the life scenarios you're working on, it can involve dozens of other people acting as relatives, friends, and coworkers.

Web lives require, first and foremost, all souls who want to participate are present and accounted for. This explains the seventy-five- to hundred-year time lapse between these types of lives. Because it is very common for members of your soul pack to be like a traveling group of theater players and switch the parts you play in your little dramas between each other from life to life, you must wait until everyone has transitioned before you can have that "Avengers assemble" moment. For example, if the souls who are your parents or grandparents in your current life want the experience of being parented by you in their next lives, everybody must wait until the entire group has transitioned before the planning can begin.

The same thing happens to pairs of souls who are committed to each other and incarnate together to work on specific life scenarios. I've seen the past lives of a number of couples who are working on a sort of rescuer theme, where they have been parent and child, siblings, and spouses and take turns either emotionally or physically rescuing each other.

Sometimes they may be family members who share a serious disease. One will die so that the other can learn how to treat the problem and survive. Then they switch places in the next life to experience the feelings the other one had to cope with.

Life themes and variations on those themes are infinite in scope. Choosing among them comes at the beginning of the planning process, so let's move on to that point. I briefly mentioned the cool computer screens we use during this time, so let's get more specific about the actual planning.

Since I grew up in the age of the rotary phone and black-and-white, antenna TV, computers continue to amaze me with the things they can do. So when I describe the screens used for life planning, remember that I see them as something out of *Star Wars*. Younger people may have a completely different perspective, so please bear with me.

After you make the initial decision to come back to earth for another life, you and your guides meet to review your karma list. Together, it is decided what you want to work on in this particular incarnation. Then it's time to convene in one of the large rooms that are always available on the other side designed for life planning. This is where the screens are located. Even though I would describe them as big computer screens, they might be more accurately called just viewing screens that are the size of a wall.

When you arrive in this space, you are met by the entities that work there. One would be me when I'm not incarnated. They can gauge your current vibrational level.

What's that you say? Sounds a little like a judgment? Au contraire, *mon frer.* As I told you before, when we incarnate for earth lives and increase our coping skills, we move up in levels, like a video game. Doing so increases our vibrational levels. Having a higher or lower vibrational level doesn't make you any "better" or "worse" than anyone else, because everyone advances at their own desired pace. And once again, no one is judging or punishing you.

Our current vibrational level is determined because that measurement will be sort of plugged into the screen wall so that only the types of life scenarios you are equipped to deal with will be displayed for you. That's right, just like on earth, no one can skip from kindergarten to their freshman year in college without doing all the work required in between. If you are not in possession of the tools you need to cope with a certain type of earth life trauma, you won't see that type of scenario appear as a possible choice on the screen.

Think of it this way. You want to be able to build a house, but you don't have a hammer or know how to use one. So you are given a piece of metal, and you must learn, first what a hammer head looks like and then how to shape the metal in that particular way. Then you are given a piece of wood, and again, you need to learn what a hammer handle looks like and then how to shape the wood into one. Once you put the pieces together, you have to learn how to use the hammer. Then you are finally ready to start building the house. Except you need to repeat the learning process with a saw, a screwdriver, any number of tools you are going to need for your construction project.

This is one of the major reasons we keep coming back. We all want a toolbox full of coping skills that can increase our vibrational levels to the point of being able to build the entire house we envisioned and earn that diploma from the earth school of hard knocks.

So our vibrational levels are determined and plugged into the wall, and that's when the fun starts. It begins slowly, with the most basic of choices. The first is gender. Once you choose male or female, other choice boxes open: straight or gay, height, weight, skin color, hair color, all of the physical attributes you will have as an adult human in the life you are planning.

From that initial choice of the male or female gender box, increasing numbers of boxes keep opening across the screen.

All relate to and depend on the choices you've already made. As you are picking what your appearance will be, actual images of you from birth to adulthood to old age appear on the screen and can be turned 360°, so you can fully examine what you will look like at every age.

I know what you're thinking because as I write this, I'm thinking, *If I saw all this gray hair and this potbelly, why didn't I edit it out when I had a chance?* That's one of the things we aren't supposed to be able to know; even psychics aren't allowed insights of that kind. We just have to trust that we did it for a reason. Some people, I think, may do some editing at this point in the process. Remember Dick Clark? He looked like a teenager his entire life!

Before the formal choosing, we will be in one of the forms that I reviewed in chapter 7. Then once everything has been picked, we usually start wearing all the physical attributes that will make up the adult appearance in our new incarnations, so we and our guides can get used to seeing us as we will be this time around.

The whole appearance-picking thing can take a considerable amount of time because some of the things you pick, like sexual identity or skin color, can have a huge impact on the things you are trying to learn. It depends on where on the planet you want to be born. Every choice you make must be examined in great detail to determine the impact it will have on your learning goals. I see the screen as being especially dynamic during this part of the process because each choice about your appearance can offer so many scenarios for learning.

The overarching lesson to be learned from all our picks is self-love. That theme is especially important in the appearance-picking phase the process. I think it's obvious that many people have been picking obesity as a way to learn self-love and acceptance. If you can learn to accept yourself as you are, while most of the people around you look down their noses, you have learned a powerful, positive lesson and gone a long way toward overcoming the feeling of being "less than" that haunts most of us.

Now that our appearance choices are made, we are ready to jump into planning the scenarios we want to encounter for learning, right? Not quite. Remember, for an "ordinary" life, whatever that may entail, dozens of other souls will interact with us. These people are planning their lives at the same time, and thanks to the amazingly sophisticated computer systems at home, all the lives are integrated so everything matches up.

If you choose to be an African American born in the United States but the people who will be your parents this time around choose to be Asian Americans, it could cause a bit of a logistical problem. But it might also present a tremendous learning opportunity and worth working out all the difficulties that may ensue.

Just as an aside, when I talk about the computer system on the other side, I don't mean there are servers, modems, and fiber-optic cables running everywhere. That kind of equipment is only necessary in this dimension. On the other side, everything—including the essences of who we really are—are just different forms of the energy supplied by the unconditional love of the Creator.

Okay. You and your soul pack have gone through the appearance-choosing phase, and everyone is satisfied with what they've chosen. So let's move on to what we are going to be doing with those bodies to enhance soul growth.

First, just as in our own little lives, there is a master plan in place for every country and, indeed, for the planet. So whatever we choose to learn must fit into the big picture. Depending on what we want to experience, we can sometimes use that larger plan to fulfill a scenario, like being killed in battle or during a terrorist attack.

I know, I know. The ever-present question of why anyone would pick that comes up. The only answer I have is it helps you in working toward that diploma, and it can help your friends and family work toward theirs by learning to cope with grief and loss without assuming the role of victim. One thing the guides have made abundantly clear is that once you allow yourself to become a victim/martyr to your feelings of grief, all learning and soul growth comes to a screeching halt. Therefore, acquiring the tools you need to prevent that are essential, not only for the life you are currently living, but for future lives as well.

It all boils down to taking your power back from any negative situation you find yourself in and using that power to increase your self-love and forgiveness. For example, when you give in to feeling like a victim, that "boo-hoo, poor me" state of mind can follow what we consider to be the loss of a loved one. You are handing over all your power to that situation to keep it alive in place of the person you think is dead.

If you stop giving your energy to that kind of negativity, it will not be able to survive because it's not real. It only seems real because you gave it energy. The more energy you give it, the more it becomes alive for you. If you let it, it may end up becoming your whole reality. You are not disrespecting a transitioned loved one by moving on with your life. They're not dead. They've moved on with their lives, so let it go. If this book does nothing else but convince a few people that death is not real, that it's only an illusion, all the time I spent writing it will be worthwhile.

Wow, how did we go down that rabbit hole? We were talking about life planning!

So we and everyone who will be incarnating with us as costars in our newest life plays have decided on our physical appearances, and we're ready to choose the things we want to work on this time around. We find ourselves back at a huge screen, but this one has the look of a *Jeopardy* answer board. Across the top are the names of the life scenarios available to us in the form we have chosen and at all our various life stages, from birth to death.

In my case, that would be a Caucasian male born in the United States, with male and female parents, siblings, wife, child, profession, and so on. Since my gender and sexual identity have been chosen previously, the number of scenarios relating to that will be limited but still numerous.

Down the side of the screen are the things from our karma list, which we compiled after our life reviews. Of course, counselors and our guides who will be with us through our incarnations are there to assist in choosing.

Usually, we pick some things from the karma list to keep working on and often one or two new things to introduce into the mix. Let's say I feel I have sufficiently developed grief coping skills from the two previous lives I wrote about before, so I'm going to focus on developing more patience and tolerance this time around.

Since I have learned to work with those two things extensively in this life, owing to the relationships I had with my mother and mother-in-law, it's a pretty safe bet they were my choices. It's also a safe bet that the lives of those two special women were constructed in such a way as to help me in my soul growth, while they also fulfilled their learning goals.

Using the demographic information and time line from the top of the board and the learning goals from the side of the board, every available scenario that could possibly play out in your life span is displayed, and you get to choose. For me, it was a screwed-up childhood, emotionally absent parents, being saved by the love of a good woman, learning about unconditional love from having a child, and so on—up to and including having this spiritual awakening in my golden years.

If you think computers in this dimension are sophisticated, imagine the one on the other side that can make all this planning come together and work! We usually listen to our guides and choose a plan that will give us what we need without too much stress and strife. But since we are making these decisions in a totally positive environment, sometimes we bite off more than we can chew.

This is why some people's lives seem to be so complicated. They may have picked too many things to try to work on at the same time, usually against the advice of their guides and life counselors. Remember the story about cow tipping? Instead of being drunk on cheap beer, when we are at home, we get sort of drunk on being immersed in a totally positive environment. As a result, we feel ten feet tall and bulletproof, like the old Travis Tritt song goes, so we think we can handle anything.

Our amnesia about what it feels like to live in the negativity of earth is akin to the amnesia about the other side that we impose on ourselves when we incarnate. That can lead to the feeling of being able to withstand anything we might encounter while incarnated.

But to get down to the specifics of picking your life scenarios, let's use myself as an example again because I so enjoy dwelling on my past. Not.

If you've read any of my other work, you know I had a complicated relationship with my mother, which I'm happy to say has been completely resolved since she transitioned. As a child, I experienced what would now be called emotional abuse, mostly of the withholding of affection kind. People of Pennsylvania Dutch extraction are not known as huggers to begin with, but because my mother read somewhere that boys who were too close to their mothers became homosexuals, a common belief in the middle of the last century, she pushed me completely away.

She also started working full time the minute I started school, and since I was about ten when my closest sibling left home, it became even easier for any type of family closeness to disappear. Since my father didn't want more children when my mother had me, he was completely emotionally unavailable from the get-go. So I was pretty much left to raise myself, out in the country with only a few neighbors for human contact.

Now before you start thinking, *Oh, poor, skinny, little, white boy, all alone in the world,* remember that my parents and I planned and agreed to all of this as a growth experience for the three of us before any of us incarnated. Even though there were times over the years that I can say I actually hated my mother, in the end, I became the one who took on the responsibility for her care when she developed Alzheimer's, and I was there as she prepared to transition to the other side.

When I heard from her after she went home, she said she really didn't enjoy the life she and I had shared much, but she lived it out of love for me and to help me learn patience, tolerance, and overcoming the emotional abuse of having your self-esteem taken away on a recurring and frequent basis. I know I've been working on those scenarios through multiple lives, as we all do. But I think this time around I've made some real progress in adding embellishments to the calligraphy of several words, and I'm pretty sure my parents did the same.

So back to the life scenario–choosing screen that I described previously. As with the appearance-choosing screen, your vibrational level will be inserted to determine the scenarios you are ready to deal with from a spiritual standpoint. The important thing to always bear in mind is that no one forces you to do any of this. If you want to change your initial choices or decide not to incarnate at all, it's entirely up to you.

If during your life planning you decide to select some special skill—for example, musical ability or artistic talent—before going into sequestration before you incarnate, you would spend some time in the various academies on the other side, where experts like artists and musicians are "in residence" when they are at home.

By learning from the experts, whatever talents you have chosen can be imprinted in your programming and develop as needed in your earth life. Ever wonder how child prodigies do the things they do? This is one way. The other way is that they were accomplished and talented people in a former life, and the subconscious memories of that come through at an early age.

Two factors are involved in all this intricate and detailed planning that can cause a deviation from what you set out to do. First, you always have free will. So just like cats with laser pointers, sometimes we come into a life and get so distracted by shiny objects that we go off on a tangent despite our spirit guides screaming in our ears.

The second factor is the impact of the incredibly negative atmosphere of this dimension on what we've planned. Everything we plan to do is conceived in the totally positive surroundings of the other side, so it's difficult to tell how scenarios will play out here. It's like baking a cake in Denver as opposed to New

York. You must adjust for the altitude, and if you don't, your cake will not turn out well. Unfortunately, life doesn't come with instructions on the side of the box for making necessary changes. You must figure them out for yourself.

Even though this entire process seems incredibly complicated, and in some ways it is, always remember that when we transition home, we regain the full use of our intellect, of which we only get to bring about 10 percent with us when we incarnate. We are surrounded by positive energy at all times, and we have guides, counselors, and access to all the accumulated knowledge of the universe to help us. So it's not overwhelming. It's also something most of us have done many times, so it's not unfamiliar territory.

In the end, we emerge from this phase with a complete plan for our next incarnation. It's been synced with all the life plans of the soul pack who will incarnate with us, and we're fired up and ready to take on the world. But (you knew there had to be a "but") hold on, Speedy Gonzales. There are a few more things we need to check preflight, so let's talk about how we do that.

13

It Takes a Village

I and authors like Sylvia Browne have described the huge central plaza we've seen when allowed to view the other side. Others may see home differently, but there seems to be somewhat of a consensus on the basic layout. I've always seen three sides of the plaza, each containing huge, Roman-style buildings with the marble columns and the whole bit. I had never seen the fourth side of the square until recently, when I was being given information for this book. The fourth side has a large, art deco–looking building with an industrial feel. I'm assuming it looks sort of like a factory because of the work that goes on there, but it might more accurately be described as a transitioning village.

This is where everyone who has a written plan for incarnating goes to wait for the appropriate time to be born and adjust their plans to what is currently happening on earth. Just like astronauts going into space, we need a place where we can be sequestered and prepared for this journey we're about to undertake. It's also not unlike being on a jury that is sequestered to prevent any news from the outside world changing the information already presented.

We've chosen everything we want to learn and how we want to learn it, so we must be sort of sealed off from access to the constantly expanding body of knowledge available to us on the other side. Once we are in this place, our only concern is about what's currently happening on the earth plane and how it will affect the lives we've planned.

After arriving at this complex, souls are taken into another screening room, where they watch a tape of the life they have planned from beginning to end to see if they want to make any changes, and, indeed, if they still want to do it at all. It's like the old buyer's remorse clause with a bank loan. Here on earth, you can take three days to change your mind; no harm, no foul. On the other side, of course, there are no time constraints, so you can change your mind about coming right up until the minute you were planning to be born.

Miscarriages, stillbirths, and sudden infant deaths often result from last-minute changes in the circumstances of the soul planning to incarnate. If things have changed on earth to an extent that the learning opportunities you were expecting to be available to you aren't going to be just right, you may decide to go back for some modifications and try again when conditions are better suited to your needs.

Of course, the miscarriage might have also been planned by the expectant parents as a way to experience that kind of grief and learning to cope with it. So, for a variety of reasons, if the life you planned doesn't feel right at this point, you can leave the village and just start over. Remember, there is no such thing as time on the other side. You may have a hundred years of earth time to make changes, depending on who you are waiting for to be ready to incarnate with you, so going back and starting over is no big deal. If you decide to continue, counselors are always available to help you make changes. But since coming to this place means you have begun your separation process for leaving home, your guides are not allowed in to help you.

I don't want to make this place sound like a prison, but we are all sequestered here after we've chosen to live another earth life and have our plans made out. We need to become reaccustomed to that negative feeling of separateness that we never have at home. It will take time in sequestration to get used to that.

The other big reason we come to this transitioning village is because things on earth are constantly changing. Imagine if it's been a hundred or so years since you last incarnated. When you transitioned home the last time, people were still riding around in horse and buggies, and radio was a new technology. Now you're coming back into a world with electric cars and instant communication with any part of the planet. You must be prepared to live in the world as it is now. Unless you end up in Amish country, like Lancaster, Pennsylvania; then you will still see people riding around in horse and buggies.

It's not like you are stuck in some sort of time warp with memories of your last earth life coloring everything you think. It's that your life plan is written around the backdrop of the time you will be born on earth, so it's a matter of your plan matching the conditions as they exist on earth at that specific time.

The other important thing that happens here is that you and your soul pack will try living in a sort of mockup village of where you will spend your adult life, so you get used to the feeling of being there. You also use this time to make sure all your costars are a good fit for the parts they will be playing.

Like all good Broadway shows, rehearsals go on for months before anyone outside the show even gets a glimpse of the production. Since you and your costars are here and together in the pre-earth life village, a lot of time is spent going over and over various life scenarios so that everyone involved can maximize their learning opportunities. A counselor will observe your interactions and may suggest two or more people change parts to make the drama play out more smoothly once everyone involved has incarnated.

Just to be clear, when everyone in the pack commits to living an earth life together, all the souls who have agreed to live out your incarnation, the actors if you will, have to be sequestered at the same time. If even one person stays outside the village a little longer than everyone else, he or she can change vibrations just enough to unbalance the whole scenario. Even though each member of the company is working on their own growth and learning, all must be on the same vibrational level for the production to be in sync and function as a whole rather than individually.

Here is where it's probably a good thing that time doesn't exist on the other side. Depending on the scenarios you pick, you may have to wait for your grandparents to be born, grow up, have children, and then wait for those children to grow up, meet each other, and have you. Conversely, if you are going to have more lives together, your grandparents have to wait until your parents' transition. Then they all must wait for you to grow old and transition. In earth years, it's a long time, but at home, it can be like the blink of an eye.

During all this waiting time, two major things happen. First, you're constantly updating your plan according to how things are changing on earth. And second, you're becoming more and more separated from home, so the complete loss of being surrounded by unconditional love is less painful when it happens at birth.

There are a lot of reasons newborn babies cry as their essences enter their bodies at birth. One of the major ones is that feeling of suddenly not being connected to all living things. Another one may be a sudden realization that he or she is reincarnating again, and who's big idea was this? Of course, the physiological reason is to get air into the lungs, so the little body can function properly, but that is only part of the whole picture.

Which brings up something interesting that I never considered until the guides explained it. Of course, after they told me about it, they were like, "Duh." Like it was so obvious. After you do all your planning and figure out who and what you are going to be in your new incarnation, you assume the adult form you are going to have to get used to being in your earth life. So how does that adult form fit into a newborn-sized body? This is where I got the "duh."

As the time of your birth in this dimension approaches, you go into a chamber that looks like a pod and start shrinking. Now, don't go around saying that I wrote we're all pod people. What I'm saying is that for our essence to fit inside a newborn, it must shrink enough to accomplish that, and it takes place in something that resembles a pod. And bear in mind that we have possession of 100 percent of our intellect while we are in the pods and still on the other side.

Until we get that earth amnesia imposed on us in the first couple years of life, we would be absolutely bored to tears, sloshing around in a uterus for nine months. So we prefer to stay in our pods. We drop in on our birth mothers occasionally to make sure everything is going as planned and feels right, but the majority of us enter our newborn bodies when we take that first breath.

All the time we're in our pods, we continue to download information about our lives' plans and any major changes in conditions on earth that might have an effect on those plans. By the time we are born, pretty much everything we need to know about our plans is in place. But through at least the first year of earth life, our essences go back and forth to the other side during sleep time for updates.

Generally, children up to the age of four or five still have a pretty open channel to the other side. They can remember past lives, see family members who have already transitioned, and have "imaginary" playmates, who are usually their spirit guides keeping tabs on things.

And so the circle of life, the real circle of life, continues. Birth, life, "death," birth into a new life, over and over ad infinitum until we learn all the things we want to learn, reach the goals we want to reach, and can finally get that diploma and graduate.

14

I Ain't Afraid of No Ghost

I promised early on to talk about ghosts, so let's delve into that subject. For something that many people refuse to believe exists, ghosts are everywhere in our culture, and not just at Halloween. There are movies about ghosts and ghostbusters (both funny and scary), TV shows about ghosts and ghost hunters, and cartoons like Casper and Space Ghost. (Yes, I know Space Ghost isn't a real ghost, but he uses the name!) One of my all-time favorites is *The Ghost and Mr. Chicken,* starring Don Knotts. All I have to hear is someone say, "Atta boy, Luther," and it cracks me up. But that's just me.

Anyway, if you visit historic places like Gettysburg, Pennsylvania, or Williamsburg, Virginia, ghost tours will take you to supposedly haunted places. Charles Dickens even let ghosts invade Christmas in the form of past, present, and future in *The Christmas Carol.* And let us never forget the Big One, the Holy Ghost. For something that isn't supposed to be real, ghosts are pretty much everywhere in our collective consciousness.

Why would that be? Why would something most people acknowledge they don't believe is real be such a common and pervasive thing in our modern world? I think it's because many people have had an experience with something they would consider paranormal but refuse to admit to themselves or anyone else that it happened. Only crazy people see ghosts. And even scarier than that, it might be a demon or the devil that you saw. Oooo, scary!

I don't want to make fun of people's fears, but one of the major goals in sharing my quest for enlightenment is to remove all the spooky/scary/demonic aspects of contact with the other side, and let people know it's the new normal. Anywhere you look on TV, there is someone in touch with the other side: *The Long Island Medium, The Hollywood Medium, The London Medium,* and thousands upon thousands of people with psychic abilities who don't have TV shows but may be well known in their local areas or on the Internet, and even people like me who are writing books.

All teach people, one at a time if we must, that no one ever dies. They just transition home, so it's not that big a deal for certain people with the ability to tune into the frequency of the vibration of the other side to see and hear what's going on there.

But let's get back to the topic of what people perceive to be ghosts. In the common vernacular, a ghost is the spirit of someone who "died" that is visible and audible to those of us still incarnated on this planet. Since we know no one ever dies—they just transition to the other side and usually take their spirits with them—how can ghosts even exist?

They can exist for a couple of reasons, and there are basically two types of them, so let me explain the difference between them.

Ghosts—or more correctly, earthbound spirits (let's call them EBSs for short)—are souls whose physical bodies have ceased to function but whose essences have not transitioned to the other side for a variety of reasons. First, they either don't realize they are "dead" or refuse to believe they are. This usually happens when death is sudden and traumatic, or when they are so attached to someone or something here on the earth plane that they can't bear to leave.

The other type of ghost the guides have told me about isn't a ghost or EBS at all, even though often perceived that way. They are small pieces of the essences left behind by those who have transitioned to keep an eye on and interact with their loved ones who are still incarnated.

If you have ever seen a *Harry Potter* movie, you know about all the portraits on the walls of Hogwarts Castle. The people depicted in them can talk to and interact with everyone in the castle. Some are even used to guard doorways and secret entrances. I guess they could be considered holograms of the real people in the paintings because they appear three dimensional and very much alive.

It's almost the same for people who have transitioned. I know it may be comforting to think Mom and Dad are just sitting in rocking chairs on a porch on the other side, passing the time watching you with rapt attention while you live out the rest of your earth life. But as I've already talked about at length, Mom and Dad are no longer the parents you knew before they transitioned. They have resumed their real lives and have things to do, places to go, and people to see. They remain interested in how you are doing and will be available to give you signs that let you know they are there, but basically, what they leave for you is sort of an interactive snapshot of the life they just experienced with you. The other, much larger pieces of them is off, resuming their normal lives.

On one of my trips with Jasper, he showed me a very long gallery-like structure where the recently transitioned could see the earth dimension and their loved ones on what looked like large viewing screens placed along the walls. Apparently, once transitioned souls decide it is time to move on, they can leave their holograms behind on the screens, which can be accessed from the earth plane.

It may seem a little gruesome, but think of it this way. I wrote previously about how we wear the adult appearance of ourselves when we are in the transitioning village, so we and those who will be sharing our incarnation with us can get accustomed to that image.

I also wrote that before we choose how we will look, we can take on one of several forms, or no form, while we're lounging around at home. So when we create these holograms of ourselves that will be recognizable to the loved ones we shared our most recent earth life with, it's sort of like taking off your clothes and hanging them up. We take off the outer appearance of ourselves from that life and leave it there, so we can be off doing whatever it is we want and need to do. I know it may sound a little like *The*

Silence of the Lambs, but things work a great deal differently on the other side. I think you've figured that out by now.

This all may seem incredibly complicated to us with the limitations of our puny human minds. But on the other side, where there are no time or space constraints like there are here, it all works.

The second type of EBS is the one more intimately involved with a place or thing here on earth. They could be most connected to what are associated with the idea of a haunting. The other side doesn't really talk much about this kind of EBS, at least in my experience. But one time in a session with Barb, when I was relating an encounter with an EBS, they mentioned the EBS is often an extension of someone currently incarnated in the place that is "haunted." In other words, the person having the encounter with an EBS actually was that EBS in a former life and brought back a piece of that specific life for some reason.

I know it seems a little confusing, even to me, but it might be that the EBS is there as a reminder of something one needs to work on from that life, like a sense of loss or a fear of some kind.

I think the disinterest that at least my guides show in the whole subject points to the relative unimportance of worrying about EBSs, but I understand people want to know about them. So I'm going to tell you about some of my experiences with them.

I can talk about four earthbound spirits I've encountered. All four were so attached to physical things here on earth that they couldn't bear to leave them.

There is a restaurant near where I live that has a beautiful nineteenth-century bar made of ornately carved wood; it has been in place for well over 120 years. It was built by the original owner of the building, which served as a tavern and inn. After I was informed by a friend that her daughter, a budding young psychic, had seen the face of a woman in her water glass and felt her presence behind the bar, I thought I should investigate.

Immediately on entering the restaurant, I saw the woman behind the bar, though no one else with me could. She wore a long, gray dress and a white apron, and 1890s' type of hairdo. She didn't have much to say other than her name was Dolly, and she had to work the bar to survive after her husband died. I didn't ask anyone who worked there if they ever felt her presence, but they may not have because she kept pretty much to herself. She seemed incredibly sad and lonely to me, more like a prisoner than a business owner. I think she was still grieving over her husband's death and feared that if she didn't work, she would lose the bar and her livelihood. I'm not sure which is stronger, Dolly's attachment to the actual bar, or her sense of loss and disbelief that her husband died and left her on her own. But whatever the reason, she's there working away, day after day.

Another earthbound soul I encountered was in the same geographical area, which because of its long history, seems to have a concentration of earthbound spirits. This time, a friend of the family told us her father had turned a window in the bedroom of his early-nineteenth-century house into a doorway, and ever since, he was having night terrors and weird dreams.

It didn't take long for me to see that the problems were coming from a man named Abraham, who owned the house at the time of the American Civil War. Abraham had been active in the Underground Railroad, and the Confederate Army was roaming around south-central Pennsylvania in the days before the Battle of Gettysburg. He and many others became fearful that the Confederates would cross the Susquehanna River on their way to attack Philadelphia and along the way, punish or kill known members of the Underground Railroad.

As a last resort, the covered wooden bridge between Wrightsville and Columbia, Pennsylvania, was burned to prevent a Confederate advance. Abraham is stuck reliving the night of the bridge burning because he was terrified Confederates had gotten across the river and were coming for him. When I talked to him, he was furious that our friend's father had turned that window into a door because, he said, Rebel soldiers could just walk right in there now. He kept waking the man up all night every night so he would watch that door and make sure no soldiers got into the house that way.

When I told Abraham that the war had been over for a long time and that he was dead and free to go home, he just snorted and walked away. Typical bullheaded Pennsylvania Dutchman. You can't tell them anything. Believe me, I grew up around enough of them to know. So he remains there, nightly guarding his house from Confederate soldiers.

More recently, my wife and I went to see Jerry Seinfeld (still funny after all these years, Jerome!) in an old theater. While waiting for the show to start, I felt an energy on the stage, sort of near the back, half behind a curtain. He was a young man with brown hair and blue eyes, dressed in a simple shirt and pants and wearing a vest. He said his name was Sean, and he was from Ireland and had worked backstage when this theater was relatively new. He showed me that a big sandbag or piece of equipment had fallen on him from high up in the rafters, and he knew he was "dead." But he loved the theater so much he didn't want to leave.

He especially loved vaudeville shows and was excited that there was a comedian playing that night. He loved comedians and said Al Jolson was one of his favorites. He also said he thought the best comedians were Jews. Maybe a little racist now, but probably not in the early twentieth century. Then the houselights went out, and he faded away to watch the show like the rest of us. So in Sean's case, he seems to know he could go home; he just doesn't want to right now. He's enjoying the theater too much.

At the same theater, waiting to see a different show, I encountered a very sad EBS named Margaret. She was wandering backstage but had never actually been in this theater when she was alive. She had owned a boarding house located on this site that was torn down to build the current structure. Her husband was killed in the Civil War. She couldn't accept his death, so she stayed there, waiting for him to come home. She was very worried that he wouldn't be able to find her since the house was no longer there.

That's my experience with earthbound spirits so far. I haven't had a lot of extra time to explore the subject further, but I do know with absolute certainty that there are no such thing as devils and demons. You are the only one who can possess your soul. The human mind can generate and believing a lot of things, so I'm fairly certain that when people encounter what they perceive as "evil spirits," they may be pieces of themselves. No matter what form we are in our basic personalities don't change that much. I've interacted with enough cranky, miserable people in this life to know that if they become earthbound spirits, they would be even more cranky and miserable, so they might enjoy doing some mean things to people.

The other side knows exactly where all these earthbound spirits are and works tirelessly to get them to transition home, which eventually they'll do. No soul is ever left behind.

15

Like Sheryl Says, a Change Will Do You Good

It may be something that comes with advancing age, but sooner or later, I think almost everyone realizes that the little play we're living out as our current incarnation comes complete with a soundtrack. If you have Sirius radio in your car, and you're old like me, your presets will undoubtedly include sixties on six, seventies on seven, and eighties on eight. Hearing all those oldies but goodies takes you back to a time in your life when things were maybe simpler, or at least seemed to be, and maybe happier, or at least remembered that way.

No matter how many thousands of times I have heard James Taylor sing any of his big hits, I still turn the radio up, close my eyes, and let the music wash over me. Advisory: if this happens to you, remember you're driving and open your eyes. I never get tired of hearing his music, and I'm not even sure why. It may be connected to something in the seventies that I don't remember, as many of us have some very fuzzy memories of parts of the 1970s. But for whatever reason, like everyone else, some songs speak to you on a soul level.

In the nineties, I became a Sheryl Crow fan like a lot of people, and I enjoyed all her music, including “A Change Will Do You Good.” It’s only recently, though, when I started taking time to really think about how my spiritual journey has changed my life for the better, that it kept popping into my head. Or, I should say, Jasper kept pushing it into my head because he wants to take credit for all my spiritual advances. By whatever means it got in there, the song title sums up perfectly what’s been happening to me, and the change has, indeed, done me really, really good.

I felt a good friend from work betrayed me and stabbed me in the back. So being true to my Pennsylvania Dutch nature, I acted like he was dead to me for about three years. Fortunately, our wives remained friends and stayed in contact, so after I had my enlightenment and realized that carrying all that anger around was not only costing me time with a friend but also hurting me emotionally, we could make amends and reconnect.

It was like the proverbial weight being lifted from my shoulders. Dragging the weight of all that anger around with me was physically demanding. I felt so much lighter after releasing it. It made me want to get rid of more burdensome fear, anger, and guilt. So I have. Sometimes a little bit at a time, sometimes a lot, but gradually, over the last three years, I managed to whittle the size of those three ugly stepsisters down to about the size of troll dolls. And believe me, before that they were Statue of Liberty size!

Again owing to my Pennsylvania Dutch DNA, I am genetically capable of passing on grudges to my offspring and hauling train cars loaded with fear, anger, and guilt with me to the grave. But due to all that I've been learning and continue to learn, I have managed to change a few genes in that DNA that will carry over to my next life.

Let me just finish by saying that I hope you have taken time to read my first three books and that they have helped you to at least start on your own spiritual journey. Do I expect you to blindly accept and believe everything I say? Certainly not. I invite you to be skeptical, and I fully expect you to have doubts and questions. If you do, that means you're open to changing your thinking concerning the things I've written about. I can only relate the things I have learned and been shown in the last three years, so please seek out the writings of other authors.

I certainly recommend Sylvia Browne and Wayne Dyer as good starting places. Go online to BarbRuhlHealing.com and take my friend Barb's course of study about the power of self. Go to YouTube, and watch videos of Esther Hicks channeling Abraham in teaching about the law of attraction. Watch Teresa Caputo or Tyler Henry on TV to see how real psychics can change people's lives by connecting with the other side.

You can never be exposed to too much information. The more you learn about anything you are interested in, but especially about spiritual growth, the easier it becomes to sort through the knowledge and determine what makes sense to you and what feels right and vibrates with your internal frequency. Once you have that foundation poured, it becomes much easier to build a belief system that works for you and houses the advancements in learning you are here for in the first place.

The size of the universe is beyond human comprehension and filled with wonders our puny human minds can't even conceive of. But while we're incarnated here, we can get glimpses of all of it by opening those minds as much as we can to the possibility of the existence of things considered spooky, wacky, or weird. To quote Shakespeare, "There are more things in heaven and earth, Horatio, than your philosophy allows." Don't be constrained by the beliefs imposed on you as a child. The only way to get the answers you seek is to question absolutely everything without fear.

If I can hope to accomplish one thing with this book, it would be to take the spooky and scary specifically out of connecting with people on the other side. Nearly all of us believe that when people "die," they go to heaven or someplace where their souls live on. Why is it such a stretch to believe we can contact them and they can contact us? They are alive, we are alive; what's the big mystery?

It may be hard for you youngsters out there to fathom, but back in the good old days before cell phones, people were not in constant contact. You had to physically locate a phone that was connected to the proper wiring to call and talk to your loved ones. We're still at that stage in establishing contact with the other side. You have to find a reputable psychic to be able to communicate directly with your loved ones at home.

Jasper recently performed an elaborate dance of the seven veils for Barb and I. Believe me, that was something you can never unsee. Jasper did this to make the point that the veil, or boundary, between earth and home is thinning, and communication between the two dimensions will become easier to accomplish as life here on earth becomes more and more complicated. That is the reason for the recent upswing of psychic awareness all over the world. The more you see it, the more acceptable it becomes, and the more normal it seems.

To conclude, I go back to my first book and pull out a quote from the poem "Desiderata": "You are a child of the universe, no less than the trees and the stars, you have a right to be here, and whether or not it is clear to you, no doubt the universe is unfolding as it should."

Despite all the hatred and turmoil in the world today, things are evolving as they should. Those of us who can, which is all of us, need to bring as much positive energy and unconditional love into this dimension as possible. How do we do that? By banishing fear, anger, and guilt from our lives. Once we accomplish that, we will truly see that, like the group Timbuk 3 sang in the eighties, "the future's so bright, you gotta wear shades." And like Sheryl Crow said in the nineties, "The change will do you good."

16 FAQs

Many times, either in conversation with friends and family or in sessions with Barb, a subject comes up that doesn't warrant the writing of an entire chapter or book, but is important enough to be discussed in a paragraph or two. For that reason, I'm going to combine several topics in this chapter, and call them FAQs.

FAQ #1: Why do children develop fatal diseases, especially cancers, at a very young age?

It's widely known among energy healers that cancer in adults is largely caused by anger, usually of the suppressed kind, and that by helping people deal with the root causes of that anger, what seemed to be an incurable cancer often simply goes away. The question then becomes, since it can take adults years of carrying around their anger to develop cancer, how can young children build up enough anger in such a short time that they would do the same? The answer is they can't and don't.

Childhood cancers, many of which are specific only to children, are planned by the parents and child before they incarnate as a way for all the parties involved to learn the coping skills required to get through that type of life scenario. Having a child with a serious illness can also serve a way of increasing the feeling of interconnectedness of the many people who will be around and aware of the situation, even if not directly involved.

If the child survives, the whole family can carry the positive feelings resulting from that through their entire incarnations. If the child transitions, the whole family must work on coping with the emotions of grief, loss, and possibly guilt. These are some of the major life scenarios we choose to work on when we come here.

FAQ #2: What's behind the fascination a lot of people have with crystals?

Crystals are used in the healing process we go through after our transition as energy boosters. They are available in many colors, each used in different ways to achieve the healing of emotional wounds we suffer while incarnated. The crystals we have on the earth plane are pale imitations of the ones that exist on the other side, but they still provide some positive energy that may help to soothe people who can tune into that type of vibration. The guides say that crystals can also help "boost the signal," as it were, of messages sent from the other side.

FAQ #3: If I plan my life in detail before I incarnate, why would I choose to go through some of the things I've had to endure?

I wrote almost a whole chapter on this subject, but since people seem to be confused about it, let me go over it again. When we are at home, we are in an atmosphere of unconditional love, and no negativity is present. That means that fear, anger, and guilt, the three emotions that are the underlying foundation of nearly all the problems we have while incarnated, are completely absent from our consciousness.

We also have an imposed amnesia about what negative emotions feel like. So no matter how much we study or read about them, we can never really learn to cope with them unless we come into the very negative atmosphere of the earth dimension and experience them first hand. Bottom line, the reason we write all these crappy things into our life plans is due to our insatiable curiosity about all things emotional and our "go ahead, dare me" attitudes. The biggest reason we do it may be the same reason people climb Mt. Everest: because it's there, and because we can.

FAQ #4: How can I get over my fear of death and dying?

That is actually a practical question because being afraid of dying is a very common fear. Controlling that fear can take a shift in the reality of the person with the fear. You must learn and internalize that death is an illusion; it doesn't exist and never has. If you can internalize that universal truth, you can move on to thinking about death as a part of life.

I realize that having any thoughts about death is abhorrent to a lot of people, so it takes a real commitment if you want to rid yourself of this fear. You must examine your fear, and figure out which part of death you are actually afraid of. Is it the not knowing the actual time and place of your death? Is it a fear that your death will be painful? Is it fear of not knowing where, if anywhere, you go after you die? Is it fear of leaving your loved ones and never seeing them again? Or is it all those things combined, which I think is the case for a lot of people.

Let's examine all those fears separately for those of you able to tease out which part of death they you the most. First, like the rest of your earth life, you planned your time and place of death before you even came here, so worrying about it doesn't make a lot of sense. You can't change it, and the veil of amnesia placed on us during our earth lives won't allow us to know the details. So it's a little like being terrified of Christmas. It's going to come on December 25 every year, whether you like it or not, and worrying about it would just suck all the joy out of the season for you and everyone around you.

Having a painful death is also a valid fear. But recent studies by medical doctors with patients who had a loss of vital signs for a time and then are resuscitated have shown that even if the patients were in extreme pain before their "deaths," during the time they had no vital signs, they had no pain at all, just a feeling of peace and tranquility.

As for not knowing where you are going after you "die," come on, really? Didn't you just read this book? And there are hundreds and hundreds of books that will tell you similar if not the same things. When we leave these physical bodies, the essence of who we are goes home, or to the other side, or to the dimension next to this one. You can even call the place heaven if it makes you feel better, but that is the only place you go. Hell, purgatory, limbo, and all those other places where so-called bad people supposedly go were made up by organized religion to scare you into going to church. They do not and have never existed.

As for seeing transitioned loved ones, I just said there is only one place we all go after leaving our physical bodies. So if they haven't already reincarnated or gone to another universe, they will be there, waiting for you.

That is a short dissertation on the reality behind what you fear. It's just a matter of wrapping your puny human mind around it and accepting it.

FAQ #5: What's with Jasper and all the costume changes?

Jasper is my primary spirit guide, for those of you who are unaware. Before I incarnated, I knew I would be born into a family of pig-headed Pennsylvania Dutch, so I would need my spirit guide to really do something outlandish to get my attention. Or I would just stubbornly ignore him. So Jasper and I came up with this idea that he would be as theatrical as possible to get my attention, as well as amuse and entertain me, while providing as much guidance as he is allowed from the other side.

In helping me with this book, he's had a lot of different looks. But the ones I think are most relevant are when he appeared as Sherlock Holmes to remind me and all of us not to overthink the whole death thing because the concept is, as he says, "Elementary, my dear Watson." The one I enjoyed the most was his performance of the theme song from the musical *Cabaret* while dressed as Liza Minelli.

He makes an excellent Liza with a "z" because they have the same eyes and original nose. But more important to the subject at hand are the words to the song, which include, "What good is sitting alone in your room, come hear the music play … put down the knitting, the book and the broom, it's time for a holiday … start by admitting from cradle to tomb, it isn't that long a stay." He's not always silly; sometimes he actually comes up with something profound, like that last quote.

The other reason he makes so many changes in his outward appearance is to remind us that no matter what we look like on the outside, we're always the same eternal soul on the inside. Whether it's the natural aging process that occurs during our earth incarnations or the many types of people we choose to become during however many reincarnations we choose to have, our sacred inner self is always the same entity.

FAQ #6: Do angels exist?

The idea of angels, or superhuman beings from the other side or another dimension, has been around for thousands of years and is not isolated to the Judeo-Christian tradition. However, in that tradition, angels have been given names, classified, and placed in a hierarchy that delegates certain jobs to the various classes of angels. It's just the typical way that organized religion can take a fairly simple idea and make it seem incredibly complicated for its own purposes.

I know volumes have been written about the existence of angels and the things they can do to help us get through rough patches in our earth lives. So if believing in angels helps you to feel closer to the unconditional love of the Creator, I say stick with your belief. I will never tell you to abandon anything that makes you feel better or comforts you. I will, however, present the reality of the situation as I've been shown it, and I encourage you to think about what you believe and take with you whatever feels right.

In all the things that Jasper and everyone else has told and shown me about the other side, I have not heard angels mentioned. And I have not seen anything that anyone on earth would consider an angel. Except, of course, for Jasper, who just showed up dressed like an angel from a 1950's school Christmas pageant, complete with a tinsel halo.

The help we receive from the other side is provided to us by our guides, both permanent and temporary, and fueled by the unconditional love they are constantly surrounded by. All the entities on the other side are there to give us any help and support that they can. They really don't care what you call them or how you choose to see them, so if you are comfortable with angels, go for it.

FAQ #7: Why do some people have quick deaths while others seem to linger for a long time?

Other than the obvious answer that we plan our "deaths" at the same time we plan our lives to be a certain way to accomplish whatever our learning purposes are, a few things can factor into what appears to be a long, drawn-out passing.

It may not seem right to us, but during a long earth incarnation, some people can build up a lot of resentment if not outright hatred toward certain family members. This can cause the person transitioning to draw out the process as a final twist of the knife before he or she leaves. If you have never experienced a loved one who could be that petty and vindictive, I congratulate you on picking a great bunch of souls with whom to share your incarnation. Many of the rest of us know that type of person all too well.

Another thing that might cause people to delay their transition is an unwillingness to let go of something or someone they are deeply attached to. I think we've all heard stories of Grandma hanging on until a favorite grandchild could reach her bedside to say that final goodbye, and that truly happens.

I'd like to relate a scenario about how people can be so attached to things on earth that they don't want to let go. This story comes from an unlikely source, my father-in-law, known to those of us who loved him as Gunk. He was a simple, hardworking man who, for whatever reason, told me things he didn't tell the rest of his family; maybe because as an outsider, I wasn't judgmental.

At any rate, a lot of the houses in the small town where he lived had backyards that extended back to an alley. Many people had small vegetable gardens in those yards, where they grew the basic tomatoes and peppers every summer. Gunk was walking down the alley one day when he saw a friend, standing at his back fence. He was looking at his little garden, where he loved to grow his favorite tomatoes. As my father-in-law got closer, his friend looked up at him and said, “Aw, the hell with it,” and took off running away from him, down the alley before he just disappeared. Gunk found out later that his friend had “died” shortly before he encountered him looking at his garden.

I know this story is true because my father-in-law wasn’t given to making things up, and even though he did enjoy his beer, this incident happened early in the day. It wasn’t until many years later, when I started to explore spirituality, that it took on real meaning for me. Now I can hold it out as a good example of a transitioning soul being so attached to something on earth that he or she has to look at it one last time and make a conscious decision to let it go.

If a person has been lingering for a while, a close loved one often tells him or her it's okay to go home, and the person will. It seems that the individual was waiting for permission before transitioning. There is that one last thread tying the person to the current incarnation. Once it's cut by whatever means necessary, he or she is able to move on.

FAQ #8: Life spans have doubled in the last one hundred to two hundred years. Will that trend continue?

The guides say yes. Even accounting for all the breakthroughs in medical treatment, the human body is slowing the aging process on its own. If you need visual proof, find a picture of your grandparents at the age of fifty, and compare it to how people now look in their fifties.

Everything in the universe is always expanding and growing, and there is really no reason people in the not too distant future could live to be 150 or 200 years old. The longer in earth years we live, the greater opportunities we have for playing out the game of life, which can greatly enhance our learning opportunities. Constant and chronic internal negativity causes our bodies to age more rapidly than necessary. As people become more interested in learning about the spiritual side of their lives, they will learn to control the fear, anger, and guilt that builds all the negativity and live longer and healthier lives.

FAQ #9: What's the deal with this "veil," and why can't I remember my life on the other side?

The veil you so often hear about is sort of like the cloak of invisibility from the *Harry Potter* movies, only instead of making you unseen, it makes you forget how wonderful life is in the negativity-free environment of the other side. The reason it's there is because if we could see home and how great it is there, we wouldn't stay here and endure all the negative scenarios we came here to learn from. People would be literally throwing themselves off bridges when things got tough here just to get to go home and start over. So in order to keep us from doing that, we give ourselves amnesia while we're incarnated. The same holds true for when we are at home and planning our next incarnation, just not quite to the same degree. That's how people end up picking crappy lives. They have forgotten how bad things can seem when we're incarnated.

FAQ # 10: I'm less afraid of my own death than I am of the death of a close loved one. How can I learn to cope with those feelings before I'm forced to by that death?

Before I answer this question, let me say up front that I'm borrowing what I'm going to tell you from my good friend Barb. She was dealing with the same issue in her own life when the guides gave her a solution. They told her to imagine the death of someone close in great detail, and by doing that, she could come to grips with the emotions that a tragedy like that would bring.

So she imagined the deaths of her parents in a number of traumatic ways, starting with hearing the news, notifying friends and family, calling the undertaker, picking out caskets, imagining the church service, watching the caskets being lowered into the graves. I think up to and including the lunch in the church basement afterward. Then she did the same for her husband and kids. By the time she imagined every possible death scenario she could think of, she knew that when the time came for these things to happen, she would be in a frame of mind to cope with and work through the grief, rather than paralyzed by it. I know it sounds gruesome and not a way most people would want to spend a sunny afternoon, but Barb says it really helps, and she's used it with her clients with good results.

FAQ # 11: If our transitioned loved ones are off planning their next incarnations or traveling around, how can they still give us messages from the other side?

The answer to that question sounds a little bizarre, but thanks to J. K. Rowling and the *Harry Potter* books and movies, I can compare it to something we're all familiar with.

When we plan our earth lives, as I've explained before, we start by choosing our gender and physical appearance. We build everything else around what we have chosen. The best analogy I can think of is that we put on a lot of makeup and prosthetics, like Robin Williams in the movie *Mrs. Doubtfire.* After we have transitioned home, we're done with that outward appearance. We won't be using it again, so we take it all off and hang it up like a used Halloween costume.

But here's the really neat part. If you've seen any of the *Harry Potter* movies, you know the walls of Hogwarts Castle are covered with paintings, both large and small, but they are more like holograms than paintings. The subjects of the pictures can move, talk, and interact with anyone looking at them. That is exactly what happens with our "outer shell," if you will, when we go home. It becomes a holographic picture of us from the life we most recently led and can interact with anyone here on earth who remembers us and wants to contact us. We may all have galleries at home filled with holograms of the many personas we have taken on during our many incarnations. That may also help to explain why we can view our past lives and learn from them with a little psychic assistance.

FAQ # 12: You only live once (YOLO) has become a popular phrase in recent years. How does YOLO fit in with the reality of reincarnation?

While the fact that we all get to live as many earth lives as we desire is undeniable, the part of that truth that makes YOLO also true is that our current incarnations are the only ones in which we assume this particular physical body and lifestyle. In other words, when choosing from all the possible variables that exist relating to an earth life, the ones that we choose will be unique to only that life. Coupled with the ever-changing conditions on earth, it means that yes, you will only live this special life in this special time and place once. The next time around, a hundred years may have passed, and you may choose to be the exact opposite of everything you were in your present life.

I know there are many more questions about these subjects and others, but there are more books in the works, and I'm learning new things all the time. Hopefully in my future publications, Jasper and I will be able to provide more answers.

Preview of

Change a Letter, Change Your Life

I was just sitting there, minding my own business like I always try to do, when I felt the presence of a new energy in my head. Ever since this journey began for me a few years ago, it's been like Grand Central Station in there, with people coming and going all the time, so I wasn't all that surprised to hear from someone new. This entity appeared as a woman in a long evening gown. She was turning boxes on a big letter board, exactly like the lovely Vanna White does on *Wheel of Fortune* every evening at seven o'clock (check your local listings).

At first, I thought it was my main spirit guide, Jasper, fooling around again because he has a propensity for playing dress-up. He makes the many costume changes my girl Cher has during a concert look weak to illustrate whatever point he's trying to get across.

He relishes making light of my puny human brain. Jasper has shown me that giving me information is like feeding a baby bird with an eyedropper, and telling me anything is like trying to teach calculus to a three-year-old. So nothing he does or anything about his appearance surprises me anymore.

But this time it wasn't Jasper in one of his many guises. It was an entirely new spirit guide. She said her name was Lorna, and she would be helping me with the writing of this book, which will be introducing the concept for a new initiative from the other side to help people incarnated on earth. The goal is that after reading the book, people will have a better understanding of one of the basic governing principles of the universe: the law of attraction.

All our friends at home—or on the other side, whichever you prefer—are always trying to help us in our earth lives by sending us messages, most of which we choose to ignore, about how the universe functions. One of the most basic principles they try very hard to get across to us is the aforementioned law of attraction.

Entire books have been written on this subject, and many authors have tried in many ways to explain how it functions and can affect our lives. But to put it simply, the law of attraction says that you get back whatever you put out there. In the vernacular of organized religion, it would be, "Do unto others as you would have them do unto you." In more secular language, it would be like attracts like. Anyway you choose to think about it, it boils down to if you put out a lot of negativity, you're going to attract a lot of negativity. Conversely, if you put out positive energy, positive energy will come back to you.

Now, you're probably asking, if all this knowledge is so well-established that it has become a universal law, what would be the purpose of the other side launching a new initiative to rehash old information? Because when we are here on earth, we choose to ignore much of the information the other side tries to sends us through our spirit guides. Plus, we have that pesky amnesia that won't let us remember most of what we know of our lives at home. For those reasons, they keep trying to tell us the same things in as many ways as possible, hoping to catch our attention.

That brings us to change a letter, change your life. What better way to repackage and reintroduce a concept than to use my and America's favorite game show? Jasper, as those of you who have read my other books already know, loves him some show business, so he is all about using the letter board to tell us that by changing one letter in a simple five-word phrase, we can win a big prize. Not a new car or a pair of ceramic dalmatians but a new outlook on life. And what, I hear you asking, is that magical phrase? It's one that we've all used time and again in our earth lives and that often colors the way we look at our life scenarios. Without further ado, that phrase is, "I believe when I see." Is there anyone out there who hasn't said some form of that at some time in their lives? Anybody? Bueller? I didn't think so.

Your sister the Tupperware hoarder is going to return the deviled egg carrier she's had since last Easter. You'll believe it when you see it. Your deadbeat cousin is going to pay back all the money he borrowed. You'll believe it when you see it. And on and on. Well, you may say, "That's just reality. That's just the way the world works." It is if you believe that it is that way. On a bigger scale, if you constantly think you never have enough money to pay the bills, then guess what? You will never have enough money to pay the bills because the universe will always match your thoughts to give you what it thinks you want.

In our new initiative, our new way of thinking, we ask our friend in the evening gown to change that W in "when" to a T. The resulting updated phrase becomes, "I believe then I see." What a difference one letter can make! It can change everything about life from a negative and stagnant approach to a positive and forward-thinking stance.

But changing that single small thing in your belief system may be one of the hardest things you will ever try to do. It means giving up your old thought processes and all your early programming, and moving fearlessly ahead into uncharted territory. Fortunately for all of us, Lorna and all the other guides are here to give us a lot of information and instruction on how to do just that.

That deviled egg carrier your sister refuses to give back? That may be a lost cause, but learning how to change your thinking so you have enough money to pay the bills every month? I think we've got that one covered. This book is going to delve much more deeply into all the things the other side is trying to show us to help us live more spiritual lives while we are incarnated, and how to use the law of attraction to our advantage. This is one old dog who can't wait to be taught some new tricks, so join me as we learn together.

CPSIA information can be obtained
at www.ICGtesting.com
Printed in the USA
LVHW03s1448100618
580220LV00002B/374/P